THE LORD OF THE RINGS
THE TWO TOWERS

PRIMA'S OFFICIAL STRATEGY GUIDE

Dan Egger

Prima Games
A Division of Random House, Inc.

3000 Lava Ridge Court
Roseville, CA 95661
1-800-733-3000
www.primagames.com

Product Development Manager: Jennifer Crotteau
Senior Project Editor: Brooke N. Hall
Editorial Assistant: Tamar D. Foster
Design and Layout: Simon Olney and Derek Hocking

ISBN: 0-7615-4194-2
Library of Congress Catalog Card Number: 2002114302
Printed in the United States of America

02 03 04 05 GG 10 9 8 7 6 5 4 3 2 1

CONTENTS

THE LEGEND OF THE RING

INTRODUCTION

You're about to take a trip through one of the most exhilarating and challenging games you'll ever play. Adapted from the blockbuster *The Lord of the Rings* movies, *The Two Towers* brings the cinematic feel and big budget special effects of these movies to your Playstation 2.

The game journeys through locations from *The Fellowship of the Ring* and *The Two Towers* films. You fight a cave-troll in Balin's Tomb, battle the Uruk-hai in Amon Hen, go toe-to-toe with Berzerkers in Fangorn Forest, and hold off hordes of Saruman's forces at Helm's Deep.

You must be skilled in both melee attacks and range attacks to make it through *The Two Towers*. You also learn how to attack quickly and repeatedly so you can score the highest kill ratings, receive more experience points, and buy new skills.

To complete the missions with each of the three main characters, you must master the melee attack of Gimli's axe, learn how to take down enemies from a distance with Legolas's arrows, and balance these two disparate styles with Aragorn.

So, before you start, check out the strategies and tactics laid out in this guide. If you play smart and purchase the right skills early on, things are easier for you at the game's end. If you get stuck, this guide will get you out of trouble and help you with step-by-step instructions. Check the maps so you don't miss a single power-up.

THE STORY

It began with the forging of the great rings.

Three were given to the Elves—immortal, wisest, and fairest of all beings. Seven to the Dwarf lords—great miners and craftsmen of the mountain halls. And nine, nine rings were gifted to the race of Men, who, above all else, desire power.

For within these rings was bound the strength and the will to govern each race. But they were all of them deceived. For another ring was made.

In the land of Mordor, in the fires of Mount Doom, the Dark Lord Sauron forged, in secret, a master Ring to control all others. And into this Ring he poured his cruelty, his malice, and his will to dominate all life.

THE ONE RING

The One Ring, an innocent-looking golden band, is by far the most powerful object in all of Middle-earth. Put it on, and the wearer becomes completely invisible. Using its powers of invisibility draws the attention of the Dark Lord Sauron, who may dispatch sinister creatures to retrieve The One Ring.

The One Ring has a strange corruptive influence, causing greed and power-lust in many who are exposed to it. Possessing The One Ring can prolong the life of its keeper, but corruption from The One Ring will eventually transform a normal Hobbit into a selfish, hideous monster.

The One Ring was forged thousands of years ago by Sauron in the fires of Mount Doom. He was close to using The One Ring's full powers to dominate Middle-earth when it was cut from his hand in battle. Sauron has been trying to reclaim The One Ring ever since losing it, and if he does, Middle-earth will be plunged into darkness and sorrow.

THE FELLOWSHIP

Gandalf discovers the true nature of the magical ring Frodo possesses and urges him to leave the Shire. Learning of Sauron's efforts to recover The One Ring, Frodo quickly escaped the Shire, dodged numerous Ringwraiths, and made his way toward the Elven stronghold of Rivendell. Here, the great leaders of Middle-earth discussed the problem of The One Ring and Sauron's recent activities. It was agreed that The One Ring must be taken to Mount Doom to be destroyed. After some debate (and an energetic but fruitless attempt by Gimli to destroy The One Ring with his axe) Frodo volunteered to bear the burden of The One Ring. Several agreed to accompany and protect him, including Gandalf, Aragorn, Legolas, Gimli, Boromir, Sam, Merry, and Pippin. Together they formed the Fellowship of the Ring and set off toward Mount Doom on their epic adventure.

THE CHARACTERS

THE FELLOWSHIP OF THE RING

The future of Middle-earth is in the hands of a few brave adventurers who have chosen to help Frodo destroy The One Ring. Each is a credit to his race, and if they are successful they can return their peoples to the peaceful lives they once knew. There are three playable characters: Aragorn, Legolas, and Gimli.

PLAYABLE CHARACTERS

ARAGORN

Men are weak, or at least this is the commonly held belief in Middle-earth. Three thousand years ago, Isildur, King of the Men of Gondor, gained great renown when he cut The One Ring from the hand of Sauron, ending his villainous reign. Soon after, however, he chose not to destroy The One Ring when he had the chance to cast it into the fires of Mount Doom. Thus, Men are known to be weak in character and not entirely trustworthy.

Aragorn can change all that. He is a Ranger, a strong man skilled in the use of many weapons, including swords, and trained to survive in every situation. Many know him as Strider, but few are aware of his true identity as son of Arathorn and heir to Isildur's throne. He is the rightful king of Gondor, and a force to be reckoned with.

Playing Style: Aragorn is a balanced character who is strong in both ranged and melee attacks.
Strengths: Aragorn is excellent in hand-to-hand combat, but can hold his own with a bow. He is agile, which enables him to quickly attack with combos.
Weaknesses: Aragorn cannot earn the same powerful arrows as Legolas, and he's not as strong as Gimli with his melee weapon.
Best Levels: He's best in levels that feature both melee and ranged warfare.

Worst Levels: Aragorn performs well in almost every type of level.
Skill-Building Strategy: Focus early on Aragorn's combos to build good scores and high experience points.
Tip: Experience is everything. Kill your enemies in groups to build your skill meter and get higher kill ratings.

LEGOLAS

Legolas is a noble Elven prince, deadly accurate with his Elven bow and knowledgeable in wilderness lore. Because he is an Elf, Legolas has exceptional sight and hearing, and although he will never die of old age, he can be hurt or killed in battle. Legolas is kind and graceful, and has a deep love for the peaceful side of nature. He and his bow attack are great assets to the Fellowship.

Playing Style: Legolas is a deadly archer who can fight through many missions with ranged attacks.
Strengths: Legolas shoots arrows more quickly and can purchase far more deadly arrows than the other two warriors. He is the most agile of the group.
Weaknesses: He has the weakest melee attacks of the three main characters.
Best Levels: Any missions that focus on ranged attacks are perfectly suited for Legolas's style of play.
Worst Levels: Levels that feature tight, close-quarters combat squelch his archery advantage.
Skill-Building Strategy: Whenever possible, build up Legolas's arrows. His most powerful arrows are incredibly useful.
Tip: Shoot offscreen and watch your skill meter. You'll often hit enemies that you might not have even seen.

GIMLI

Gimli is a stubborn dwarf who makes up for his lack of height and grace with great strength, bravery, and tenacity. Gimli fears nothing when he has his trusty axe in hand, and his temper makes him formidable when angry. His gruff disposition keeps him from easily making friends, but as a member of the Fellowship he is a tough and loyal ally. Gimli dislikes Elves; but, during his adventures with the Fellowship he develops an unlikely friendship with Legolas. Gimli is proud of his heritage, and looks forward to seeing his cousin in the Mines of Moria.

Playing Style: Gimli is what gamers often call a "tank." He's slower than the others (especially when using his ranged attack), but more powerful. He's best when fighting a horde of enemies.

Strengths: Gimli is a great character for those who like to mash buttons. Even his quick attack is powerful and reaches a long distance. If you don't want to learn a bunch of ranged attack strategies, stick with Gimli.

Weaknesses: Gimli is slower than the others, and takes a long time to unleash his ranged attack. His combos take a while to build up. Expect to be parried often.

Best Levels: Levels in which the enemy keeps coming in a small, confined area.

Worst Levels: Levels that require a lot of ranged attacks.

Skill-Building Strategy: Build up Gimli's health and attack upgrades to withstand more enemy attacks.

Tip: When playing as Gimli, start your attacks farther back from your enemy to give Gimli time to build up his attack.

ISILDUR

Isildur is a playable character in the first level. If you beat one of the secret levels with any player, you open a fully charged level 10 version of this powerful character.

Playing Style: Isildur is a balanced character who plays like Aragorn.

Strengths: Isildur is already charged up to level 10 and has all of the skills that Aragorn can purchase.

Weaknesses: Like Aragorn, Isildur's balance means he cannot match Legolas in archery, or Gimli in brute strength.

Best Levels: He slices though almost any level.

Worst Levels: Isildur doesn't have any worst levels.

Skill-Building Strategy: Isildur's skills are already at the maximum level.

Tip: Use the combos named after Isildur to build your meter and score perfect kills.

NONPLAYABLE CHARACTERS

FRODO

Frodo is the Ringbearer, a brave Hobbit whose cleverness keeps him alive in the face of danger. His Uncle Bilbo left him The One Ring, along with the troubles that accompany it. However, Frodo shows great resistance to the sinister powers of The One Ring. He has volunteered to take it to Mount Doom and destroy it forever for the good of Middle-earth. There could not be a more difficult task.

GANDALF

Gandalf the Grey is known and respected throughout Middle-earth as a wise man and a great conjurer. He is not young, but he can use staffs and swords skillfully in combat. Nevertheless, Gandalf's strength lies in his vast repertoire of magic spells and abilities. He is the only character capable of using magic, and he uses it well.

Gandalf serves as a father figure to Frodo, providing leadership and protection to the young Hobbit. He would carry The One Ring himself, but his knowledge of magic is too dangerous to expose to the corruptive powers of The One Ring.

THE FORCES OF EVIL

THE UNDERLINGS

You face a wide variety of dangerous enemies during this adventure; the more you know about each enemy, the better your chances of beating them. Here is a quick guide to all your foes.

GOBLIN

Strengths: The Goblins are fast and agile. They tend to stay in groups.
Weaknesses: They are not heavily armored and they're easy to kill.
One-Shot Kill: Goblin Bane
Most Dangerous When: They hit you as a large group. One at a time, these Goblins are not dangerous, but in numbers they can hurt you.
Tips: Use your combos to take out a few of these at a time and build your skill meter. Use speed attacks.

GOBLIN WITH SHIELD

Strengths: Like the regular Goblins, these guys hop around. They're also shielded, making them tougher to kill.
Weaknesses: After you take down their shields, they aren't threatening.
One-Shot Kill: Goblin Bane
Most Dangerous When: Pestering you among a group of other enemies.
Tips: If you face a group of Goblins and one of them has a shield, take out the shield first, then combo together a series of kills. Use fierce attacks.

ORC MELEE

Strengths: When spinning with its two blades, this creature can slice through your defenses.
Weaknesses: Without a shield, this Orc is open to ranged attacks.
One-Shot Kill: Orc Bane
Most Dangerous When: Together with several other Orcs, especially when a couple of them have shields.
Tips: Parry to stop his momentum, then take out with speed attack or combo.

ORC WITH SHIELD

Strengths: His shield protects him against speed attacks. His long trident weapon can trip you up from a distance.
Weaknesses: After the shield is gone, this Orc isn't tough.
One-Shot Kill: Orc Bane
Most Dangerous When: You try to keep a combo going. If you don't throw in a move to disarm his shield, he stops you cold.
Tips: When this Orc approaches in a group, take out his and any other shields first. When they're gone, focus on the other enemies. Use fierce attacks to break shield.

ORC ARCHER

Strengths: His flaming arrows can hurt and pester you from great distances.
Weaknesses: He can be killed by a single fierce blow.
One-Shot Kill: Orc Bane
Most Dangerous When: Launching arrows at a distance while you fight other enemies.
Tips: Use your ranged attacks to take these guys out early. Their arrows move slowly, so you have a brief time to dodge or parry.

URUK-HAI MELEE

Strengths: They are stronger than Orcs and have long weapons that can hit you from a distance. Armored versions of these troops are hard to hurt.
Weaknesses: They can be beaten by strong frontal attacks.
One-Shot Kill: Bane of Saruman
Most Dangerous When: You are trying to get off the ground or run away.
Tips: Face up to these large enemies and use your fierce attacks and combos to take them down. Knock them to the ground, then stab down with R2.

URUK-HAI CROSSBOWMEN

Strengths: Their arrows are not that dangerous, but they also carry grenades that light the ground on fire wherever they hit. If you step into this fire, you'll be badly hurt.
Weaknesses: They aren't tough against melee attacks.
One-Shot Kill: Bane of Saruman
Most Dangerous When: They drop an explosive grenade at your feet and you've got nowhere to run.
Tips: Stay clear when you see the grenades hit, and pick these guys off from a distance.

URUK-HAI BOMBER

Strengths: The explosive charges that they carry are deadly.
Weaknesses: They are susceptible to all attacks.
One-Shot Kill: Any ranged attack will do.
Most Dangerous When: Charging you while you're fighting other enemies.
Tips: In levels where you face these guys, watch them, and hit them early to keep them at a distance. You can use them against their own troops.

URUK-HAI SCOUT

Strengths: The Uruk-hai Scouts are stronger and deadlier than Orc troops. Plus, they carry a long sword that can hit you from a distance.
Weaknesses: Uruk-hai scouts are lightly armored, and because of this, they are more susceptible to your attacks than regular armored Uruk-hai.

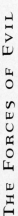

THE FORCES OF EVIL

One-Shot Kill: Bane of Saruman.

Most Dangerous When: Attacking you in groups.

Tips: Because you'll face several Uruk-hai scouts at once, stay on the outside of your attackers so you can focus on one target at a time. Don't fight them all at once.

BERZERKER

Strengths: This enemy has a long reach and can parry almost all of your attacks.

Weaknesses: The Berzerkers don't have shields, so they can be stopped with arrows. Also, they attack in a pattern that is easily figured out and countered.

One-Shot Kill: Any weapon that sets its target on fire.

Most Dangerous When: You're focused on someone else.

Tips: When a Berzerker enters a battle, take him out first. Dodge as he goes into his looping, double-swing attack, then counter when he misses. Use R2 to finish him off if you knock him down.

CAVE-TROLL

Strengths: These guys are huge and carry a mace that can take away much of your life in a single swing.

Weaknesses: They aren't bright. Use the same tactic to kill them, even when they are with other cave-trolls.

One-Shot Kill: Any weapon that sets its target on fire.

Most Dangerous When: They are always dangerous, but when they join other enemies in a battle, they should be your first priority.

Tips: Attack these creatures by hitting them with your fierce attack, escaping as they try to smash you, then hitting them again. Repeat this until they fall.

FOREST TROLL

Strengths: Forest trolls are strong and, unlike cave-trolls, they can venture from the darkness of an underground lair. The can also throw chunks of wood at you from a distance, and they can't be hurt by ranged attacks.

Weaknesses: Like cave-trolls, forest trolls aren't bright. Even if you face more than one of them, you can take them out with a little patience.

One Shot Kill: Any charged-up melee attack that lights them on fire.

Most Dangerous When: They have you trapped with nowhere to run.

Tips: Be patient and methodical. Strike with a fierce attack, dodge their counterattack, then hit them. Don't get greedy and try to hit with too many shots at once.

RINGWRAITH

Strengths: They cannot be harmed by regular weapons.

Weaknesses: They are susceptible to fire.

One-Shot Kill: None

Most Dangerous When: They can keep you from getting to fire.

Tips: Don't get between two Ringwraiths. Always stay on their outside, and strike at one at a time.

THE BOSSES

In some missions, you must fight a difficult boss after you've made your way through several underlings. Here are all the toughest ones, and a quick guide on how to beat them.

THE WATCHER IN THE WATER

Gates of Moria Level: At the end of this level, you face the Watcher in the Water. This multi-tentacled beast can cause you serious trouble if you don't know how to beat it.

Strategy: Block the Watcher's tentacles when they attack you. When you do, they'll stick straight up in the air, and you can cut them off with a speed or fierce attack. This causes the Watcher's head to pop out of the water, where you can hit it with your ranged attack.

Extra Tip: Parry a couple of its attacks before chopping off a tentacle. If you do this, your attack will be less risky.

CAVE-TROLL

Balin's Tomb Level: After killing many lesser Orcs in Balin's Tomb, you face the cave-troll. He's not bright, but when he grabs a chain as a weapon, he's dangerous.

Strategy: Hit the cave-troll with several fierce attacks when he first appears. Your character then jumps up on a ledge in a cutscene. From this position run along the ledge, dodging his attacks, and shooting him with ranged weapons. Do this until he dies.

Extra Tip: Watch your health and ammo while on the upper ledge. If you run low on either, a lesser Orc may join you and bring you the power-up you need. But you'll have to kill him first.

LURTZ

Amon Hen Level: This Uruk-hai is a master archer and a deadly swordsman. You must outthink him to beat him.

Strategy: After beating him in an archer's duel, lure him toward one of the stone pillars at the map's end. He strikes at you and gets his sword stuck in a pillar. Take a couple of fierce shots at him, then run to the next pillar and trick him again. Repeat this until you kill him.

Extra Tip: Use combos when he's stuck to boost your skill rating and increase the your fierce attack's damage.

WARG RIDERS

Gap of Rohan Level: Both the Wargs and their riders are deadly. You have to outsmart both to defeat them.

Strategy: After you kill all of the Wargs, approach the Sharkû and stay several yards in front of him. He charges and you can dodge or parry. Eventually the Warg rises on its hind feet. Use your fierce attack and strike its underbelly. Do this several times to kill both the Warg and its rider.

Extra Tip: Parrying the Warg charge is easier than dodging. Even if you get knocked to the ground, you take little damage if you parried.

THE CONTROLS

HANDLING THE GAME

Knowing your controls is crucial to success in *The Lord of the Rings: The Two Towers*; you must be familiar with every button and command. Here's a breakdown of all the basics.

SPEED ATTACK ✖

The speed attack lets quickly swipe your enemy. It does not do as much damage as the fierce attack, but it is faster. It doesn't break shields.

Alternate control option: Move the right control stick ⇦ and ⇨ for a speed attack.

FIERCE ATTACK ▲

The fierce attack hits your enemy with a solid blow. It can break shields that try to stop it.

Alternate control option: Move the right control stick ⇧ and ⇩ for a fierce attack.

KNOCK BACK ●

Hit this button to push enemies away to avoid their fire. In level 10, you can use this button to push down ladders.

Alternate control option: Push down the right analog stick for a knock back.

PARRY ■

This button enables you to defend yourself against enemy attacks and to block arrows.

Alternate control option: You can also hit R1 to parry.

KILLING MOVE R2

Hit this button when your opponent is on the ground to finish him off with a killing blow.

JUMP BACK L2

Escape attacks by hitting this button and jumping out of your enemy's range.

EQUIP RANGE WEAPON L1

Pull this trigger to prepare your ranged attack. While holding this down, you can aim your shot.

FIRE RANGED WEAPON L1 + ✖

While holding L1, push down on ✖ to draw back your ranged attack weapon. The longer you hold down ✖ the more powerful your attack will be. Release ✖ to fire.

BASIC COMBINATION MOVES

When you start *The Lord of the Rings: The Two Towers* you have all of the level one skills. Some of these are your basic combo moves. Learn them well.

THREE-HIT SPEED COMBO ✖, ✖, ✖

This triple shot hits your target quickly and scores you several skill-earning hits in a short time.

DOUBLE HACK ▲, ▲

This combo knocks down or kills most of your early enemies. It's great for taking on big enemies like the cave-troll.

BASIC MOVES THAT MUST BE PURCHASED

LINKED ATTACK ■, ✖, R2

Start with a successful parry, and follow it with a speed hit and a killing move. You can purchase skills that make this a one-shot kill move for different kinds of bad guys.

DEVASTATING ATTACK—HOLD ▲ AND RELEASE

Charge up your fierce attack, then release it when your weapon is glowing and your enemies are near. The effect is deadly.

GAME SCREEN AND MENUS

KNOWING YOUR HUD

All the important information you need while playing *The Two Towers* is displayed on your screen. At a glance, you can spot the exact status of your character and his mission. Here's a brief primer on the heads-up display.

HEALTH METER

Keep this full; when it runs dry, you are dead. If it runs low, pick up a health power-up to recharge your health.

POWER-UPS

GREEN HEALTH POTION

This fills your health meter.

RED HEALTH POTION

This partially fills your health meter.

ELF-STONE

This adds points to your experience meter.

EXPERIENCE METER

This gauge fills as you gain experience by killing enemies and picking up Elf-stones. When it completely fills, you reach a new level.

SKILL METER

This is an important gauge. As you kill enemies and avoid hits, your skill meter grows. The higher this skill meter, the better your kill rating.

When you are at full skill meter, you score perfect kills. A full skill meter also adds damage to your attacks and gives you double experience for each kill.

KILL RATINGS

You receive a score for each kill based on your skill meter when you finish off your enemy. Higher kill ratings equal higher experience point scores.

FAIR

You earn little experience for these kills.

EXCELLENT

You hit one or two of these on your way to perfect.

GOOD

Decent, but not what you want.

PERFECT

You get double the experience and a weapons boost.

MISSILE GAUGE

This gauge tells you how many ranged attack arrows (or axes) you have left. Your ammo limit is determined by which character you're playing.

CRUCIAL INFORMATION

Sometimes a new gauge appears in the upper-right corner of your screen. These show crucial mission information, and each is fully explained in the walkthrough text.

SKILL UPGRADES
THE STRATEGY THAT MATTERS

Picking the right skill upgrades is as important as the best gameplay tactics. Smart use of your experience points makes your life easier when you reach the difficult levels.

Skill upgrades are purchased with the experience points you earned while playing through a level. At each level's end, the Missions Results screen appears. Here your points are tallied according to each of your kill ratings.

When the game is done tallying your score, two numbers appear on the screen. In the screen's lower-middle, you'll see how many experience points you earned during the last level.

The upper-right side shows how many total upgrade points you have available. This carries over points that you didn't spend during the last round.

Before you spend your points, remember these three tips:

1. Don't buy every upgrade available. If you don't need it, don't buy it. Save points for the next round.
2. Buy only the skills you will use. If you rarely use combos that include the parry button, don't waste upgrade points on a combo that uses that button.
3. Buy skills that fit your character. Focus on skills that max out Legolas's arrows, Aragorn's combos, and Gimli's health meter.

ARAGORN SKILLS

LEVEL ONE

TRIPLE STRIKE
Cost: NA
Use: ✕, ✕, ✕
Note: A fast combination, effective against smaller, unshielded enemies.

DOUBLE HACK
Cost: NA
Use: ▲, ▲
Note: A damaging combination to smash through obstacles or shatter enemy shields.

SHADOW STRIKE
Cost: NA
Use: R2
Note: This thrust finishes off any knocked-down foe.

COMBAT KICK
Cost: NA
Use: ●
Note: Knocks enemies away from you and out of striking distance.

SWORD PARRY
Cost: NA
Use: ■
Note: Blocks enemy attacks and projectiles.

DÚNEDAIN BOW
Cost: NA
Use: Hold L1, then press and release ✕.
Note: This is Aragorn's starting ranged attack weapon.

LEVEL TWO

RUSH ATTACK
Cost: 3,000
Use: ✕, ●
Note: Charge forward and drive unshielded enemies to the ground.

RISING ATTACK
Cost: 8,000
Use: ✕
Note: Attack as you regain your feet, taking enemies by surprise.

ISILDUR'S SWIFT TERROR
Cost: 5,000
Use: ✕, ✕, ▲
Note: An effective combo for taking out unshielded foes.

ISILDUR'S WAR RUSH
Cost: 5,000
Use: ✕, ●, R2
Note: Wound, knock down, then finish off powerful enemies with this combo.

RANGER'S FURY
Cost: 2,000
Use: ▲
Note: A devastating attack. Press and hold ▲ to use.

STRENGTH OF THE STEWARDS
Cost: 10,000
Use: Automatic
Note: Permanently increases your health.

LEVEL FOUR

GOBLIN BANE
Cost: 4,000
Use: ■, ✕, R2
Note: Instantly kills a goblin (lesser Orc).

CHARGE ATTACK
Cost: 4,000
Use: ✕, ●
Note: Charge forward from long range to drive unshielded foes to the ground.

ISILDUR'S DEATH CHARGE
Cost: 5,000
Use: ✕, ●, ▲
Note: Wound, knock down, and strike your enemy with this combination attack.

ISILDUR'S GAMBIT
Cost: 5,000
Use: ✕, ▲, ✕, ✕
Note: Use this combo to strike an unshielded foe, dispatch him, then quickly strike another.

ROHAN'S BOW
Cost: 4,000
Use: Hold L1, then press and release ✕.
Note: Fired like those from the Dúnedain Bow, the barbed arrows of the Rohirrim cause serious damage.

STRENGTH OF ISILDUR
Cost: 10,000
Use: Automatic
Note: Permanently increases your health.

LEVEL SIX

ORC BANE
Cost: 6,000
Use: ■, ✕, R2
Note: Instantly kills an attacking Orc.

ISILDUR'S DELIVERANCE
Cost: 5,000
Use: ▲, ✕, ✕, ▲
Note: Effective for rapidly dispatching shielded enemies.

STRENGTH OF ELENDIL
Cost: 10,000
Use: Automatic
Note: Permanently increases your health.

WILDERNESS RAGE
Cost: 4,000
Use: Hold down ▲.
Note: A more devastating charged attack.

MASTER SWORDSMAN
Cost: 10,000
Use: Automatic
Note: Increases the damage of your speed attack.

LEVEL EIGHT

BANE OF SARUMAN
Cost: 8,000
Use: ■, ✕, R2
Note: Instantly kills an attacking Uruk-hai.

ISILDUR'S JUDGMENT
Cost: 5,000
Use: ▲, ▲, ●, ▲
Note: Use against a powerful foe to smash his shield, knock him to the ground, and strike him.

STRENGTH OF THE ARGONATH
Cost: 10,000
Use: Automatic
Note: Permanently increases your health.

WRATH OF NÚMENOR
Cost: 6,000
Use: Hold down ▲.
Note: A devastating charged attack that sets fire to multiple foes.

GONDOR BOW
Cost: 6,000
Use: Hold L1, then press and release ✕.
Note: The iron arrows of Gondor cause terrible damage.

LEGOLAS SKILLS

LEVEL ONE

TRIPLE STRIKE
Cost: NA
Use: ✕, ✕, ✕
Note: A fast combination, effective against smaller, unshielded enemies.

DOUBLE HACK
Cost: NA
Use: ▲, ▲
Note: A damaging combination to smash through obstacles or shatter enemy shields.

SHADOW STRIKE
Cost: NA
Use: R2
Note: This thrust finishes off any knocked down foe.

COMBAT KICK
Cost: NA
Use: ●
Note: Knocks enemies out of striking distance.

KNIFE PARRY
Cost: NA
Use: ■
Note: Blocks enemy attacks and projectiles.

MIRKWOOD LONGBOW
Cost: NA
Use: Hold L1, then press and release ✕ to fire.
Note: This is Legolas's starting ranged attack weapon.

LEVEL TWO

RUSH ATTACK
Cost: 3,000
Use: ✕, ●
Note: Charge forward and drive unshielded enemies to the ground.

ELROND'S SWIFT TERROR
Cost: 5,000
Use: ✕, ✕, ▲
Note: An effective combo for taking out unshielded foes.

ELROND'S WAR RUSH
Cost: 5,000
Use: ✕, ●, R2
Note: Wound, knock down, then finish off powerful enemies with this combo.

ELVEN FURY
Cost: 2,000
Use: ▲
Note: A devastating attack. Press and hold ▲ to use.

FORCE OF CELEBORN
Cost: 10,000
Use: Automatic
Note: Permanently increases your health.

RIVENDELL LONGBOW
Cost: NA
Use: Hold L1, then press and release ✕ to fire.
Note: Fired like those of the Mirkwood Longbow, the ash arrows of Rivendell cause more damage.

LEVEL FOUR

GOBLIN BANE
Cost: 4,000
Use: ■, ✕, R2
Note: Instantly kills a goblin (lesser Orc).

RISING ATTACK
Cost: 8,000
Use: ✕
Note: Attack as you regain your feet, taking enemies by surprise.

CHARGE ATTACK
Cost: 4,000
Use: ✕, ●
Note: Charge forward from long range to drive unshielded foes to the ground.

ELROND'S DEATH CHARGE
Cost: 5,000
Use: ✕, ●, ▲
Note: Wound, knock down, and strike your enemy with this combination attack

ELROND'S GAMBIT
Cost: 5,000
Use: ✕, ▲, ✕, ✕
Note: Use this combo to strike an unshielded foe, dispatch him, then strike another.

LOTHLÓRIEN LONGBOW
Cost: 6,000
Use: Hold L1, then press and release ✕.
Note: The enchanted arrows of Lothlórien do ghastly damage.

LEVEL SIX

ORC BANE
Cost: 6,000
Use: ■, ✕, R2
Note: Instantly kills an attacking Orc.

ELROND'S DELIVERANCE
Cost: 5,000
Use: ▲, ✕, ✕, ▲
Note: Effective for rapidly dispatching shielded enemies.

DRAGONFIRE ARROWS
Cost: 8,000
Use: Hold L1, then press and release ✕.
Note: These magical arrows set your enemies on fire.

FORCE OF GALADRIEL
Cost: 10,000
Use: Automatic
Note: Permanently increases your health.

GIL-GALAD'S RAGE
Cost: 4,000
Use: Hold down ▲.
Note: A more devastating charged attack.

LEVEL EIGHT
BANE OF SARUMAN
Cost: 8,000
Use: ■, ✕, R2
Note: Instantly kills an attacking Uruk-hai.

ELROND'S JUDGMENT
Cost: 5,000
Use: ▲, ▲, ●, ▲
Note: Use against a powerful foe to smash his shield, knock him to the ground, then strike him.

MITHRIL ARROWS
Cost: 10,000
Use: Hold L1, then press and release ✕.
Note: These arrows penetrate and damage all enemies in their path.

ELVEN BOW MASTERY
Cost: 10,000
Use: Automatic
Note: Increases the damage of each arrow you fire.

GIMLI'S SKILLS
LEVEL ONE
TRIPLE STRIKE
Cost: NA
Use: ✕, ✕, ✕
Note: A fast combination, effective against smaller, unshielded enemies.

DOUBLE HACK
Cost: NA
Use: ▲, ▲
Note: A damaging combination to smash through obstacles or shatter enemy shields.

SHADOW STRIKE
Cost: NA
Use: R2
Note: This thrust finishes off any knocked down foe.

AXE THRUST
Cost: NA
Use: ●
Note: Knocks enemies away from you and out of striking distance.

AXE PARRY
Cost: NA
Use: ■
Note: Blocks enemy attacks and projectiles.

EREBOR AXES
Cost: NA
Use: Hold L1, then press and release ✕.
Note: This is Gimli's starting ranged attack weapon.

LEVEL TWO
RUSH ATTACK
Cost: 3,000
Use: ✕, ●
Note: Charge forward and drive unshielded enemies to the ground.

BALIN'S SWIFT TERROR
Cost: 5,000
Use: ✕, ✕, ▲
Note: An effective combo for taking out unshielded foes.

BALIN'S WAR RUSH
Cost: 5,000
Use: ✕, ●, R2
Note: Wound, knock down, then finish powerful enemies with this combo.

DWARF FURY
Cost: 2,000
Use: ▲
Note: A devastating attack. Press and hold ▲ to use.

MIGHT OF ROCK
Cost: 10,000
Use: Automatic
Note: Permanently increases your health.

MIGHT OF IRON
Cost: 10,000
Use: Automatic
Note: Permanently increases your health.

LEVEL FOUR
GOBLIN BANE
Cost: 4,000
Use: ■, ✕, R2
Note: Instantly kills a goblin (lesser Orc).

CHARGE ATTACK
Cost: 4,000
Use: ✕, ●
Note: Charge forward from long range to drive unshielded foes to the ground.

RISING ATTACK
Cost: 8,000
Use: ✕
Note: Attack as you regain your feet, taking enemies by surprise.

BALIN'S DEATH CHARGE
Cost: 5,000
Use: ✕, ●, ▲
Note: Wound, knock down, then strike your enemy with this combination attack.

BALIN'S GAMBIT
Cost: 5,000
Use: ✕, ▲, ✕, ✕
Note: Use this combo to strike an unshielded foe, dispatch him, then strike another.

RUNE OF PROTECTION
Cost: 10,000
Use: Automatic
Note: Permanently increases your health.

LEVEL SIX
ORC BANE
Cost: 6,000
Use: ■, ✕, R2
Note: Instantly kills an attacking Orc.

BALIN'S DELIVERANCE
Cost: 5,000
Use: ▲, ✕, ✕, ▲
Note: Effective for rapidly dispatching shielded enemies.

MIGHT OF BALIN
Cost: 10,000
Use: Automatic
Note: Permanently increases your health.

MIGHT OF GLÓIN
Cost: 10,000
Use: Automatic
Note: Permanently increases your health.

MORIA AXES
Cost: 4,000
Use: Hold L1, then press and release ✕.
Note: Thrown like Erebor axes, the razor-sharp Moria axes cause even more damage.

MOUNTAIN RAGE
Cost: 4,000
Use: Hold down ▲.
Note: A more devastating charged attack.

LEVEL EIGHT
BANE OF SARUMAN
Cost: 8,000
Use: ■, ✕, R2
Note: Instantly kills an attacking Uruk-hai.

BALIN'S JUDGMENT
Cost: 5,000
Use: ▲, ▲, ●, ▲
Note: Use against a powerful foe to smash his shield, knock him to the ground, then strike him.

MIGHT OF THE KHAZAD-DÛM
Cost: 10,000
Use: Automatic
Note: Permanently increases your health.

WRATH OF MORIA
Cost: 6,000
Use: Hold down ▲.
Note: This devastating attack sets fire to multiple foes.

AXE MASTERY OF KINGS
Cost: 10,000
Use: Automatic
Note: Increases the damage of your fierce attack.

TACTICS

THE 10 ESSENTIAL GAMEPLAY TACTICS

The Two Towers is a challenging game, but if you use smart tactics, you'll make it through like a pro. Here are the 10 most important tactics to remember:

YOUR KILL RATINGS MATTER.

At first glance, you might think that kill ratings are just a way to make you feel better about your gameplay skills, but they are important. You earn more experience points for each "perfect" kill than you earn for a "fair" kill.

Get a feel for building up your skill meter early, so you can practice getting perfect kills before you reach the difficult levels. The more experience points you get, the better the skills you can purchase, and the better you'll perform in the next rounds.

REPLAY EARLY LEVELS IF YOU DON'T SCORE WELL.

If you complete an early level with only a "good" rating, hit the replay button on the lower-left side of your Mission Results screen and try again. It takes time to play this level over, but if you get more experience points with an "excellent" or "perfect" score, you'll have far fewer replays of later levels.

You can progress to the end without gathering much experience, but it's worth it to take extra time in the beginning to avoid the difficulty at the end.

DON'T WASTE EXPERIENCE POINTS ON USELESS SKILLS.

If you don't use certain button combos in a battle, and you still get through the levels with excellent or better ratings, don't waste skill points on unnecessary combos.

For instance, if you don't like stringing together ■, ✕, R2 for Goblin Bane, don't purchase Orc Bane or the Bane of Saruman. Passing up those two saves 14,000 experience points that could be used maxing out your favorite combos, weapons, and health.

PURCHASE COMBOS WITH SIMILAR BUTTON COMMANDS.

Most of the attack combos named after Isildur/Elrond/Balin offer different variations of ✕ ▲. When you purchase several of these

combos, mash away at these two buttons and you'll often hit one of the combos.

When you have them all, you will easily hit combo after combo, and rack up numerous perfect kills. It's an effective melee strategy.

DON'T WORRY ABOUT HEALTH AND AMMO.

One of the best design features in this game is that your enemies drop power-ups when you need them. The game senses when you

are low on health or ammo, then gives you what you need.

Because of this, concentrate more on killing your enemies than keeping your health meter full. This is especially true in huge battles; you'll take damage often, but find health more often.

DON'T GET DISTRACTED BY ARCHERS.

Take out archers before you wade into a melee battle. If you can't, don't let them distract you.

When you join close-quarters combat, ignore the archers. Their arrows cause less damage to you than enemy melee attacks, and you'll block many arrows by accident. Some enemy arrows will even injure your foes.

KNOW YOUR CHARACTER'S STRENGTHS.

How you approach each confrontation should be dictated by the character you're playing. For instance, Legolas can take out groups of

enemies from a distance with his arrows, while Gimli has to wade into the middle of a battle.

You can't approach one level the same way with all three characters. When you learn their nuances and strengths, you can take each of them to the game's end.

KNOW YOUR WEAPONS AND SKILLS.

Don't purchase a new skill if you won't use it. Pause the game every once in a while and check your upgrades to see if you're using everything you've earned.

Sometimes, when you purchase a special weapon, such as Legolas's *mithril* arrows, you find that the entire game has changed. It would be awful to play your regular style of game when you could dominate your foes with a new weapon or skill.

DON'T OVER-THINK YOUR BATTLES.

Your skill meter rises when you attack with speed and use combos. It doesn't reward pretty moves and well-thought-out gambits. So, jump into the action and let your button fingers take over.

If you try to figure out the best combo for each situation (shielded foe, for instance), your skill meter drops. Instead, plow into your enemy and let the chips fall where they may. Pretty soon the right combos become instinctive.

USE .

Many players forget this useful button, but L2 will save your life many times if used correctly. When facing large bosses or groups of enemies, L2 gets you clear and gives you time to regroup.

This button is useful in the secret missions. When you are surrounded by eight Uruk-hai warriors, this button gives you the space and distance you need to survive.

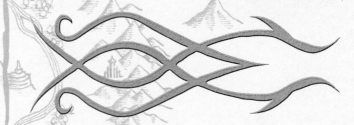

MISSION INTRODUCTION

LEVEL-BY-LEVEL GUIDE

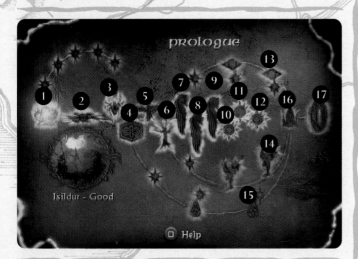

For the next 16 sections, this guide walks you through each level in *The Two Towers*. For the levels in which all three of the characters follow a similar playing style, we give a general strategy and point out specific tactics that work for each character.

For the levels that require each character to lean on his own strengths, we break those guides into sections for each character. Considering how unique the experience is for each character, we recommend playing through with all three.

Even if you skip some walkthrough sections, check out the skills strategy at each chapter's end. These suggestions will help you make efficient use of your experience points.

LEGEND

1. Prologue
2. Weathertop
3. Gate of Moria
4. Balin's Tomb
5. Amon Hen
6. Fangorn Forest
7. Plains of Rohan
8. The Westfold
9. Gap of Rohan
10. Helm's Deep—The Deeping Wall
11. Helm's Deep—The Breached Wall
12. Helm's Deep—Hornburg Courtyard
13. Secret Mission—Aragorn
14. Secret Mission—Legolas
15. Secret Mission—Gimli
16. Secret Mission—Isildur
17. Codes

LEVEL 1: PROLOGUE

GOALS

- SURVIVE
- LEARN YOUR BASIC ATTACK AND DEFENSIVE MOVES

PLAYABLE CHARACTERS

ISILDUR

ENEMIES

ORC WITH SHIELD   ORC MELEE

The first level in *The Lord of the Rings: The Two Towers* serves two purposes. It introduces you to the world and story behind *The Lord of the Rings*, and it teaches the fighting system basics.

Orc entrance point

mt. doom

LEGEND
- elven archers

lava floe

lava floe

MORDOR

You start in the middle of a cutscene. Be prepared to fight when the action turns from movie images to game graphics.

You can parry (■) if you like, but you can make your way through this first bit without getting hit all that much. Later you can practice parrying.

The first lesson the game covers is how to use speed attacks. When you're facing an enemy that doesn't have a shield, hit ✖ to make a speed attack.

After you go through the first batch of bad guys, more descend. A cutscene plays, then it's back to the action.

To practice, continue pressing ✖ to launch more speed attacks and take out more enemies. To build up better kill ratings, use combos such as ✖, ✖, ▲ and ✖, ▲, ✖, ✖ to vanquish more foes.

TIP

Don't stand against the Orcs' entrance points. You won't be able to see what they're doing to counter their moves.

Start building excellent and perfect kill ratings by using your combos correctly, aggressively pursuing new kills, and avoiding getting hit by bad guys.

The fierce attack is the object of this lesson. When you face an enemy with a shield, press ▲ to shatter that shield with a fierce blow.

After you are proficient at parrying enemy attacks, mix in your newly learned defense with some offense. You need both, because the Orcs are more aggressive in this section, and you have to take them down.

You can also use combos during this short stage, but for the most part, you can string together several perfect kill ratings if you act quickly and stay out of the enemy's reach.

When you finish, Sauron comes to the foot of Mount Doom and Isildur defeats him in a cutscene. Your work is done—for now.

Skill Upgrades

You won't be able to purchase skill upgrades after this first level. Pay attention to what you buy after the other levels. If you wisely pick skills, you'll have an easier time getting through the game.

Mount Doom erupts, but you don't have more than a moment to appreciate the scenery. More Orcs are on their way. Be careful of falling lava.

This section is good for practicing parrying (■). Even if you're beating your enemies at this stage, practice. Later it will save your life.

LEVEL 2: WEATHERTOP

GOALS
- PROTECT FRODO
- LIGHT ALL FIVE RINGWRAITHS ON FIRE

PLAYABLE CHARACTERS

ARAGORN

ENEMIES

RINGWRAITH

LEGEND
 relight your torch

campfire

weathertop

WALKTHROUGH

This is a short level, good for developing your parrying skills. Your role is to protect Frodo Baggins from the Ringwraiths, who have hunted him down, and to kill the Ringwraiths.

When the level starts, a Ringwraith faces you. Attack him with your lighted torch. Normal weapons cannot injure Ringwraiths. You must use fire.

Take out this enemy with a combination of parrying and fierce attack. Alternating between ■ and ▲ eliminates the Ringwraith.

If your torch goes out because the Ringwraith hit you, run to the campfire in the middle of the map, hit ✗, and return to the action.

TIP
Relight your torch. You want your skill meter to remain full so that you earn a perfect kill rating when you finish off the Ringwraith.

When you kill the first Ringwraith, a second one follows. Dispatch this one as you did the first. Keep an eye on your torch to make sure it's lighted.

A short cutscene plays, and another Ringwraith makes an appearance. Frodo puts on The Ring to disappear.

CRUCIAL BATTLE INFORMATION

While you're playing, a health meter appears on the right-hand side of your screen. This meter shows Frodo's health. Don't let it go down to zero.

When the cutscene ends, you face another Ringwraith. Use both parry and fierce attack (■ and ▲) to build skill points so you can achieve a perfect kill rating.

When you kill the third Ringwraith, another cutscene plays and two more Ringwraiths show up. One stabs Frodo. You cannot stop him.

When the gameplay starts again, you take on the two Ringwraiths. Watch Frodo's health meter; if you take too long to eliminate the Ringwraiths, he will die and you'll fail the mission.

After the first is dead, check your torch to make sure it is flaming, then take out the last one.

When you fight the two Ringwraiths, concentrate on one enemy at a time. If you lose focus, you may end up getting between the two of them and find yourself badly damaged in short order.

You've saved Frodo. Now things are going to get tougher.

Take care of the first one by keeping him between you and the other Ringwraith.

Skill Upgrades

Your next mission requires fighting a larger number of enemies. Purchase Isildur's Swift Terror so you can use this combo to build your skill meter.

Aragorn

Purchase: Isildur's Swift Terror
Cost: 5,000
Use: Hit ✕,✕,▲ to unleash this deadly combo.
Reason: Isildur's Swift Terror builds your skill meter in the midst of battle.

LEVEL 3: GATE OF MORIA

GOALS
- FIND THE GATE OF MORIA
- SLAY THE WATCHER IN THE WATER

PLAYABLE CHARACTERS

ARAGORN   LEGOLAS   GIMLI

LEGEND

start	starting point	🔑5	Battle 5	treasure chest (arrows)
🔑1	Battle 1	🔑6	Battle 6	treasure chest (Elf-stone)
🔑2	Battle 2	🔑7	Battle 7	treasure chest (health)
🔑3	Battle 3	🔑8	Battle 8	treasure chest (green health)
🔑4	Battle 4	🔑9	Battle 9	boss battle

waterfall

the path to the
gate of moria

BRIDGE

watcher

gate

start

ENEMIES

GOBLIN   **ORC ARCHER**

ARAGORN STRATEGY

Aragorn is the most balanced of all the warriors, so you can use either ranged attacks or melee attacks. In this level, you'll build higher skill ratings with melee attacks and combos. Use Isildur's swift terror, which you purchased after last level, to build your skill meter toward perfect kill ratings.

WALKTHROUGH

This is the first full adventure level you tackle in *The Two Towers*; use it to test your skills. You must know the basics well to make it through alive; to play through with a good rating, you must master some expert skills.

BATTLE 1

As you round the first corner, Orc troops drop in front of you.

You must defeat three Goblins. None of them have shields, and they aren't extremely aggressive. Take the battle to them to increase your skill meter.

BATTLE 2

As you move forward, two more Orcs pop out from behind the wall. Dispatch them quickly and move on. As you step forward, a few more attack you while you're crossing a short bridge.

BATTLE 3

After you cross the bridge, more Orcs attack. You should easily fight through these.

TIP

Quickly move from battle to battle so that you can keep your skill meter high and achieve better kill ratings.

ITEM!

In a crevice on the left side of the path lies a treasure box. Use ✕ to open it with your melee weapon.

Continue past the crevice and down the path. Soon the camera angle changes and a short cutscene plays.

LEVEL 3: GATE OF MORIA

BATTLE 4

When the movie sequence ends, you face Orc soldiers and archers. Use ■ to deflect the flaming arrows as you approach the ground troops.

Two Orcs drop into the path between you and the archers. While blocking arrows, eliminate the two Orcs with quick attacks.

excellent

Advance safely and quickly and take out the Orc archers on the ground. Use combos such as ✗, ✗, ✗ to gain extra skill points and get a higher kill rating.

TIP

If you purchase an attack combo after a mission, use it in the early parts of a new mission. The difficulty usually ramps up quickly, so practice while you can.

When you're done, hold down ⌊L1⌋ and hit ✗ to use your ranged weapon. Aim carefully with your left joystick and fire when the archer above you has a white marker over his head.

When you are done with these Orcs, continue down the path. Go across a narrow bridge, and another cutscene kicks in.

LEGOLAS STRATEGY

Because of Legolas's superior range attack abilities, you can take down many of the orcs from a distance. Attack as many as possible, or your skill meter and kill ratings will stay low.

BATTLE 5

When the movie sequence finishes, you face another set of Orc archers. Shoot them with your ranged weapon, then move forward to attack the ground troops.

As you advance, more Orcs climb up from the left side of the cliffs below you. Take them down.

ITEM!

A treasure box sits on your right-hand side, past the archers' standing spots. Open it using ✗.

excellent

Continue farther and more Orcs jump at you from the left. Attack them to earn points.

BATTLE 6

Several Orc archers fire on you. As you advance toward them, several more drop behind you.

Take out the nearby Orcs and build up your skill meter. Keep your guard up, and block incoming arrows. They'll knock down your skill meter.

GIMLI STRATEGY

Gimli is effective in fighting situations like the ones in this level. Although he is not as good as the others with ranged weapons, he can take out the Orc archers with ease.

BATTLE 7

When you round the next corner, there are two Orcs on the ground and two archers behind them. Get rid of the two nearest Orcs first.

Now the two archers behind them demand your attention. Shoot the one on the right with your ranged weapon while blocking shots from the second.

When the first is dead, pick off the second from a distance. Quickly make your ranged shots to build your skill meter.

BATTLE 8

You reach the edge of a lake. Continue walking until two Orcs pop out of the water.

Kill them, and move forward until two more Orcs jump out of the water. Kill them as well.

Move forward again to battle with a host of Orcs. Fight your way through.

If you make your attacks speedy, you build up to excellent and perfect kills.

SECRET

In the middle of the action, watch for an Orc standing waist-deep in the water ahead of you.

When he's not looking, a long tentacle from the Watcher grabs him and pulls him under.

BATTLE 9

Push forward until you face several Orc archers. Parry their arrows while fighting Orcs on the ground, then return fire with your ranged weapon.

Attack and watch for attacks from your left side. Sometimes Orcs pop in from offscreen to cause you trouble.

ITEM!

In the corner next to the final Orc archers is a treasure box. Open it with your melee weapon. It is often a health power-up. You'll need that soon.

Now proceed; another cutscene plays. This one introduces the game's first boss, the Watcher in the Water. The Watcher takes out your partner, so you have to beat it on your own.

CRUCIAL BATTLE INFORMATION

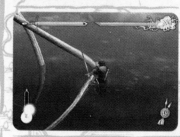

When the watcher appears, a second health bar pops up on the upper-right side of your screen. This is the watcher's health meter. When it dwindles to nothing, you've beaten him.

BOSS BATTLE

The Watcher is a large creature with three tentacles that can badly hurt you. Your first responsibility is to block its attacks using ■. You can use either fierce or speed on the tentacles after they are stunned.

You don't want it to knock you down several times in a row. If you don't parry the first shot, this can easily happen.

TIP

Individually parry each attack. If you just hold down ■, the Watcher's second and third shots will hit you.

When you successfully parry an attack, the tentacle stands straight up in the air.

Just because one or two tentacles reach upward doesn't mean that the others won't keep attacking. Always be prepared to parry.

When it's dead, the level is over and you can continue on your way.

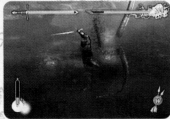

Run toward one of the tentacles sticking up and use ▲ for a fierce attack. This chops off the tentacle.

Skill Upgrades

When you're done with this level, you'll earn enough experience points to purchase some useful skills.

Your next mission requires you to fight a horde of enemies on the ground, then a huge cave-troll using your ranged weapon. Prepare accordingly with these basic suggestions.

When you lop off a tentacle, the Watcher lifts its head above the surface.

Aragorn

Purchase: Ranger's Fury
Cost: 2,000
Use: Hold down ▲ to charge your sword and release for a powerful attack.
Reason: This power helps you clear out large masses of Orcs in the next level.

When the Watcher's head is above the surface, fire a shot with your ranged weapon to hurt it.

Legolas

Purchase: Elrond's Swift Terror, Rivendell Longbow
Cost: 5,000, 4,000
Use: Elrond's Swift Terror (✕, ✕, ▲) enables you to build your skill meter, and the Rivendell Longbow makes your arrows more powerful.
Reason: You need the combo to take out Orcs, and the arrows help you vanquish the cave-troll.

Stay knee- to waist-deep in the water and repeat the process of parry, fierce attack, and ranged attack until you reduce the Watcher's health bar to nothing.

Gimli

Purchase: Balin's Swift Terror, Dwarf Fury
Cost: 5,000, 2,000
Use: The first (✕, ✕, ▲) is a valuable skill-building combo, and the second (hold ▲) enables Gimli to charge up his axe for deadly attacks.
Reason: These help Gimli increase his melee strength so he can build experience.

TIP

Don't stand too deep in the water. You'll lose mobility and you won't have a good view of all three tentacles. Attack and retreat over and over.

THE LORD OF THE RINGS
THE TWO TOWERS

LEVEL 4: BALIN'S TOMB

GOALS
- FIGHT OFF THE INVADING ORCS
- SLAY THE CAVE-TROLL

PLAYABLE CHARACTERS

ARAGORN   LEGOLAS   GIMLI

LEGEND
  ranged attack ammo

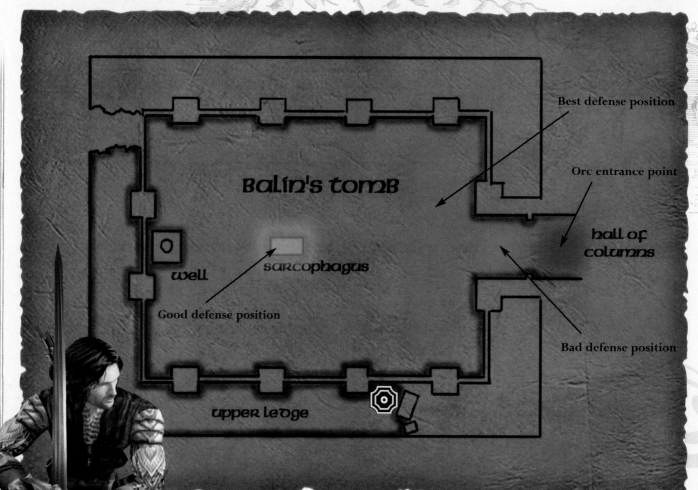

BALIN'S TOMB

Best defense position

Orc entrance point

hall of columns

well

sarcophagus

Good defense position

Bad defense position

upper ledge

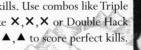

ENEMIES

GOBLIN

GOBLIN
WITH SHIELD

CAVE-TROLL

WALKTHROUGH

Balin's tomb is a short but intense battle that tests both your melee and ranged attack skills. You face an onslaught of Goblins followed shortly by a tough battle with a cave-troll.

NOTE
Each of the three playable characters should approach this level differently, so we cover each segment from each character's perspective.

PART 1
ARAGORN

This is a good level for Aragorn. His swordsmanship serves him well against the flood of enemy troops. Start by watching the door from the Hall of Columns.

Stand away from the entrance and attack when the Orcs rush in. String together combos to quickly build your skill meter to its highest point.

Isildur's Swift Terror (✕,✕,▲) is useful for building up your skill meter.

When you score a perfect kill and your skill meter is maxed out and glowing, try for quicker kills. Use combos like Triple Strike ✕,✕,✕ or Double Hack ▲,▲ to score perfect kills.

TIP
Perfect kills give you the most experience points, and it's hard to get your skill meter full. Get as many as possible before your meter runs down to zero.

Keep your back to the other members of the Fellowship. They can take care of themselves.

This is where you'll make the most of your experience points, so get as many kills as you can.

LEGOLAS

This is one of the best maps for Legolas. If you purchased Elrond's Swift Terror (✕,✕,▲) you'll glide through the first part of Balin's tomb.

Complete Elrond's Swift Terror several times to build your skill meter.

If you do this, you'll string together a few perfect kill ratings, thanks to Legolas's speed and mobility.

Use simpler attacks when your skill meter is fully charged. Don't waste time trying fancy moves.

TIP

Don't stand too close to the door where the Orcs enter. If you block their path, they wait in the distance, and your kills won't add up.

You might be tempted to rely on Legolas's ranged attack, but don't. Although he's a powerful archer in other levels, this battle is too cramped for his bow to be useful.

Attack the shield-carrying Orcs with ▲. You can build your skill meter with combos, but they are easier to handle without their shields.

GIMLI

You'd think a powerhouse like Gimli would have an easy time in a level like this, but you're wrong. This is one of his tougher levels.

Because Gimli is not as quick as the other two characters, skill and timing are crucial.

TIP

Keep your eyes open for health power-ups when your health meter runs low. You have to turn your attention away from the battle for a moment to find what you're looking for.

Don't get fancy. If you take time to develop a combo, you'll get hit. Stick with the basics (✗,✗,▲, ✗,✗,✗, and ▲,▲).

Parry telegraphed attacks and take out enemy shields with fierce attacks. When they're gone, you'll plow through the rest.

PART 2

After you've fought awhile, a new combatant interrupts the battle—a massive, angry cave-troll.

CRUCIAL BATTLE INFORMATION

when the cave-troll appears, a second health bar pops up on the upper right-hand side of your screen. Take it down to nothing.

ARAGORN

When the cave-troll enters Balin's Tomb, check your health. You want it high, because when you significantly hurt the cave-troll, you'll move upstairs away from the power-ups on the ground.

As Aragorn, you can easily fight the cave-troll on the ground. To start, avoid his first attack.

When he swings with his massive mace, run toward him and attack him twice with your fierce attack (▲, ▲).

Immediately hit L2 to jump back to safety.

Wait until he swings again to injure him in a few swings.

GIMLI

Gimli follows a similar strategy. Despite his smaller size, he can get out of the way by double-tapping L2.

> ## TIP
> *To score extra experience points, take out the Orcs running on the ground; watch for the cave-troll.*

LEGOLAS

If you're playing Balin's Tomb as Legolas, you have to beat the cave-troll in a different way. Here, Legolas's agility is more useful than the L2 jumping dodge.

If you try to dodge the cave-troll's attacks using L2, you'll get hit. Instead, run in, make a single fierce attack, then run out of his attack range.

Make your attack count, but be patient. Don't try a double attack. If you do, he'll get you.

> ## TIP
> *Keep your health up during the entire first part of the troll battle. There are health power-ups everywhere.*

PART 2

After you injure the cave-troll, your player jumps on the upper ledge of the tomb in a short cutscene. The cave-troll ditches his mace for a more dangerous chain whip.

ARAGORN

The cave-troll whips at you with the chain. A Goblin hops on the ledge with you. Take the Goblin out first.

When the Goblin is gone, concentrate on the cave-troll. At the beginning of your battle, hide on one side of the columns. If the cave-troll is on the other side, you're safe from his attacks.

When he attacks on the wrong side of a column, quickly launch two ranged attacks at him and run out of the way.

Eventually, he tears away the columns. You can't use this strategy forever, but make the most of it while you can.

When he tears away some of the middle columns, adjust your strategy. Run from side to side on the upper ledge. Stop when his attack misses you, and launch an arrow at him.

Get a feel for how many arrows you can launch at a time. Don't get greedy. It's better to hit him with too few arrows and escape safely than it is to hit him with more and take damage.

If you run out of ammo, look to the upper ledge's far right (see the map) to find more ammo.

Patiently chop the cave-troll's health meter. Watch for Orcs that jump onto the ledge. They won't hurt you much, but they'll set you up for a shot from the cave-troll.

It takes a lot of arrows, but you'll kill this massive beast.

GIMLI

The last part of this level takes more patience if you play as Gimli. He can handle the Orcs that join him on the ledge, but he can't unload ranged attacks as quickly as the other guys.

You can take down the cave-troll with Gimli if you don't mind slowly doing it. Run from one side of the ledge to the other and fire a single axe when the cave-troll tries to whip you.

Keep an eye on Orcs, and you'll whittle the cave-troll down to nothing. An axe in the heart is as good as an arrow.

When the cave-troll dies, head to the next level.

LEGOLAS

This part of the level isn't easy, even for a ranged weapon master like Legolas. The big problem is that he has difficulty quickly handling minor Orc attacks.

Because Legolas doesn't have the same melee strength as the other two, it takes him longer to kill enemies. The cave-troll takes advantage of these extra moments.

Attack the Orc with Elrond's Swift Terror (✕, ✕, ▲) when the Orc attacks you. Hopefully you'll take him out with a single combo.

After you eliminate the Orc, the cave-troll is easy work. Move back and forth along the ledge, reload your ammo, and hit the cave-troll with three or four arrows at a time.

Watch for more Orcs. If you see one in the distance, hit it with a combo or an arrow while you move toward it. That makes it harder for the cave-troll to hit you.

SKILL UPGRADES

Your next mission requires you to fight enemies on the run and many archers. Here's what you should pick up.

ARAGORN

Purchase: Isildur's Gambit, Rohan Bow
Cost: 5,000, 4,000
Use: Hit ✕, ▲, ✕, ✕ to unleash the powerful Isildur's Gambit. The Rohan Bow automatically increases your arrows' strength.
Reason: Isildur's Gambit is similar to Isildur's Swift Terror, so you can miss one combo and still hit another.
Note: These choices assume that you've reached level four. If not, choose Rising Attack.

LEGOLAS

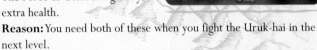

Purchase: Elrond's Fury, Force of Celeborn
Cost: 2,000, 10,000
Use: Elrond's Fury enables you to charge your swords for an attack. The Force of Celeborn gives you extra health.
Reason: You need both of these when you fight the Uruk-hai in the next level.

GIMLI

Purchase: Might of Rock
Cost: 10,000
Use: Might of Rock adds to your life meter. Gimli can purchase several of these upgrades, so start early.
Reason: Because Gimli has a slower attack, he takes more damage and needs more health.

LEVEL 5: AMON HEN

GOALS

- SLAY AT LEAST 75 ORCS
- RESCUE FRODO BEFORE HIS HEALTH METER RUNS OUT
- FIND BOROMIR BEFORE HIS HEALTH METER RUNS OUT
- SLAY LURTZ

PLAYABLE CHARACTERS

ARAGORN   LEGOLAS   GIMLI

the seat

start

fallen
head
statue

1

2

foot
bridge

3

4

5

6

the ruins

amon hen

7

bridge

lurtz
battle arena

LEGEND

1	Battle 1
2	Battle 2
3	Battle 3
4	Battle 4
5	Battle 5
6	Battle 6
7	Battle 7
⚔	treasure chest (arrows)
⊡	treasure chest (elf-stone)
✳	boss battle

ENEMIES

URUK-HAI
SCOUT

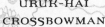
URUK-HAI
CROSSBOWMAN

LURTZ

WALKTHROUGH

Amon Hen is a tough level. You fight a horde of deadly Uruk-hai troops, and you must kill at least 75 to make it through.

BATTLE 1

You start at The Seat, and you're surrounded by Uruk-hai troops. How you take them down depends on who you're playing.

> ### NOTE
> *Each of the three characters has vastly different strategies for playing through Amon Hen. We discuss these strategies in detail here.*

ARAGORN

If you're playing as Aragorn, build your skill meter to its peak by attacking with quick combos.

Make sure you're not too far away from the action, but also protect your back.

You'll build up a set of perfect kill ratings and be off to a great start on your experience point collecting.

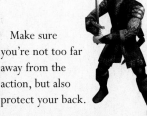

As you leave The Seat, you're attacked by a couple more Uruk-hai. Take them out as well.

TREASURE CHEST

On top of The Seat is a treasure chest containing an Elf-stone.

LEGOLAS

Legolas can use his arrows efficiently in this level. When the first battle starts, jump to the corner behind Aragorn and Gimli and unleash arrows.

Constantly lock onto a new target. If you chain together a long string of hits, you'll get perfect kill ratings.

GIMLI

As Gimli, dive into the action, using combos to build your skills. Wade into the midst of the battle striking with Balin's Swift Terror (✗, ✗, ▲).

LEVEL 5: AMON HEN

CRUCIAL BATTLE INFORMATION

on the upper-right side of your screen, two new power meters appear. one has a uruk-hai face with a number below it indicating how many uruk-hai you need to kill.

on the right of that meter is frodo's health meter. it drops slowly as you progress through the level. if it dwindles to zero, you fail the mission.

BATTLE 2

The Uruk-hai start searching for Frodo. Go after them, but don't rush. Watch his health meter; you have plenty of time.

ARAGORN

A group of Uruk-hai troops is in front of you, supported by crossbowmen in the distance.

Pick off the crossbowmen in the distance. They can hurt your attempts to build up your skill meter, so nail them with a ranged attack.

When they're down, take out the remaining Uruk-hai, building your skill meter as you go. Head toward the footbridge.

TREASURE CHEST!

Before you reach the footbridge, look left for a treasure chest. Open it using ✕ and grab the arrows within.

When you pass under the footbridge, Uruk-hai swarm you. Unleash Isildur's Swift Terror to score a couple more perfect kills.

TREASURE CHEST!

On top of the footbridge, there is a treasure chest containing an Elf-stone.

As you progress, three more crossbowmen appear in the distance.

Take them out with ranged attacks, then use your swords to kill the Uruk-hai beyond them. Watch out for the crossbowman on the statue farther down the path. He'll cause you problems if you're not careful.

LEGOLAS

Use Legolas's superior ranged attack skills to pick off Uruk-hai crossbowmen at a distance, but in hand-to-hand combat, attack with Elrond's Swift Terror (✕,✕,▲) to build your skill meter.

Shoot arrows ahead of you as you play through. If you shoot an arrow and your skill meter increases, you've hit a target.

LEVEL 5: AMON HEN

GIMLI

Don't fight the archers from a distance. Jump into the action and take them out up close and personal. However, if an archer shoots at you from an area you cannot reach, back up and chop him down with your throwing axes.

BATTLE 3
ARAGORN

Three Uruk-hai crossbowmen spring an ambush. This gets ugly because they throw explosive charges with flames that burn you.

The crossbowmen lay down fire on either side of you. If you step into this fire you'll be burned. Immediately step behind the wall between you and the Uruk-hai.

From this location, attack the Uruk-hai with deliberate and safe ranged attacks.

Or, wait for the fires to burn down, then take off. With Aragorn, it's better to run. You'll score better kill ratings down the path using your sword.

LEGOLAS

With Legolas, you can easily take out all three bombers. Stay behind the wall, peek out, and pierce them with arrows.

GIMLI

Gimli's best strategy is to skip this battle. Even if you have to run through the flames to do it, it's worth it because you get better kill ratings with melee attacks.

BATTLE 4

Frodo is hiding as a bunch of Uruk-hai passes him. Check his health meter when the game starts.

ARAGORN

Drop into the ruins and face an Uruk-hai crossbowman. Take him out from a distance, then eliminate the other Uruk-hai near him.

LEVEL 5: AMON HEN

TREASURE CHEST

When you descend the first stairs to the ruins, there is an ivy-covered arch. Cut the ivy and enter the secret room to get a chest containing an Elf-stone.

Drop to the ruins' lower level to battle more Uruk-hai, including three crossbowmen. Take care of the crossbowmen if you can, but focus on the melee warriors to get the best kill ratings.

When you're done at the ruins (even if there are a few crossbowmen left), go down the stairs and rejoin the other characters. Slay the two Uruk-hai they are fighting.

LEGOLAS

Kill the first cross-bowman from long distance. After getting rid of the Uruk-hai that were on his level, step down to the next level and stand near the stairs.

From here you can fight Uruk-hai with your melee attack and shoot the off-screen crossbowmen when you have a moment. You can rack up some high kill ratings with your arrows and swords.

GIMLI

Take it to the enemy with Gimli, and don't worry about the cross-bowmen. Clear out the accessible Uruk-hai.

BATTLE 5

ARAGORN

You and the other two characters end up on a bridge surrounded by Uruk-hai. You have to kill enough of them to get the counter on the upper-right side of your screen to zero before Frodo's health meter goes to zero.

After you kill all 75 Uruk-hai, Frodo escapes with the help of a few arrows.

You can fight a few extra Uruk-hai on the bridge to gain more experience points, but watch the meter on your screen. You need to find Boromir in time.

When you're ready, continue past the bridge to the last battle at the end of this map.

LEGOLAS

Start with your swords, and when the Uruk-hai on your side are dead, use your arrows to help your fellow characters.

GIMLI

Use Balin's Swift Terror to chew through the Uruk-hai forces. When you're done with the ones on your side, help your partners.

BOSS BATTLE

Having lost Frodo, Lurtz is looking for a fight. He's an excellent archer and swordsman; be careful.

ARAGORN

You start with a ranged weapon showdown. The best technique for Aragorn is to dodge the arrows rather than parry them.

Dodge and fire a single arrow, then repeat this strategy to nail Lurtz with eight arrows.

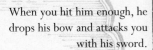

When you hit him enough, he drops his bow and attacks you with his sword.

Rather than fight this monster, run from him to one of the stone pillars. Turn and parry his attacks if he gets too close.

If you're standing close to a pillar when he swings at you, dodge. He'll miss and stick his sword in the pillar. Now you can attack him. Use your best combo (✗,✗,▲ or ✗,▲,✗,✗) to cause the largest amount of damage.

Watch for random Uruk-hai who join the battle. They are a distraction, but they bring you health. Take care of them so the distraction doesn't linger.

Lure Lurtz toward the pillars and attack him when his sword gets stuck. You'll take him out quickly this way.

When you're done, join the others and mourn Boromir's death.

LEVEL 5: AMON HEN

37

LEGOLAS

With Legolas, you can quickly get through the first segment. His arrows are more deadly, and he can easily parry Lurtz's shots.

Dodging Lurtz during the swordfight is difficult, and the roaming Uruk-hai that join the battle are problematic. Stick to the outside and lure Lurtz into hitting the columns.

GIMLI

Dodge the arrows from Lurtz and quickly launch a counterattack. Lurtz fires faster than Gimli, so concentrate on evasion.

When you are melee fighting against Lurtz, you'll realize he is faster than you. Because of this, stay close to the stone pillars and use L2 to jump out of danger. Running away won't cut it.

SKILL UPGRADES

You are boosted to level four skills this time. Your next mission involves powerful enemies, so bring out the big guns.

ARAGORN

Purchase: Rising Attack, Strength of Isildur
Cost: 8,000, 10,000
Use: Tap ✕ when you get knocked down to hit your attacker as you rise with a devastating attack.

Reason: In the next level, you face powerful enemies who knock you down. Use this to make them pay.
Note: If you have enough experience points left over, use them to pick up Strength of Isildur. If not, save your points and get it in the next round.

LEGOLAS

Purchase: Rising Attack, Lothlórien Longbow
Cost: 8,000, 6,000
Use: Tap ✕ when an enemy knocks you down and you'll strike as you rise with a devastating attack.

Reason: In the next level, you face powerful enemies who knock you down. Use this to make them pay. Lothlórien Longbow increases the strength of your arrows, which is especially helpful in the next level.

GIMLI

Purchase: Rising Attack, Balin's Gambit
Cost: 8,000, 5,000
Use: Tap ✕ when you get knocked down to hit your foe as you rise with a devastating attack. Hit ✕, ▲, ✕, ✕ to strike multiple foes with Balin's Gambit.

Reason: The Rising Attack helps you counterattack, and Balin's Gambit helps you earn experience points.

LEVEL 6: FANGORN FOREST

GOALS
- DEFEAT THE ENEMY
- DEFEAT THE FOREST TROLLS

PLAYABLE CHARACTERS

ARAGORN   LEGOLAS   GIMLI

LEGEND

1	Battle 1	7	Battle 7
2	Battle 2	8	Battle 8
3	Battle 3	9	Battle 9
4	Battle 4	✱	Treasure chest (Elf-stone)
5	Battle 5	⊞	Treasure chest (health)
6	Battle 6		

the path through

fangorn forest

ancient tree

9

8

7

cave

6

fallen log

2

orc camp

3

4

5

waterfall

start

1

waterfall

ENEMIES

GOBLIN

GOBLIN
WITH SHIELD

ORC ARCHER

BERZERKER

FOREST TROLL

LEGOLAS

Use your swords, not your arrows in this instance. Elrond's Swift Terror scores big here.

GIMLI

Attack and parry when necessary. Take out the shields first, then unleash Balin's Swift Terror.

WALKTHROUGH

The level begins in Fangorn Forest. While your enemies are not as numerous here as in other levels, they are difficult foes.

BATTLE 1

ARAGORN

As you start down the path, Orc troops ambush you. Take out the shields first, then kill the rest to pick up good kill ratings.

BATTLE 2

ARAGORN

Step into a large hollowed-out log and face a Berzerker. These enemies are tough, so carefully approach.

It takes a lot of shots to kill the Berzerker, so be patient. Attack with your fierce attack; even though he parries every shot, you'll build your skill meter.

When your skill meter is full, back away from the Berzerker. He attempts to attack you with long, sweeping strikes of his sword. Use L2 to jump back twice, then attack him when he pauses at the end of the attack.

Eventually you knock him down or he dies. If he's not dead, use your killing stroke **R2** to finish him. Keep building your skill meter so you get more experience for the kill.

TIP

Whenever he knocks you to the ground, hit ✖ to strike him with a vicious Rising Attack (if you've purchased that skill).

When you're done with the Berzerker, head to the end of the fallen log, use your sword to cut away the tree in your path, then continue.

LEGOLAS

Legolas has an advantage against the Berzerker. His arrows are deadly and fire rapidly. Stay back and shoot when you get a clean shot.

If he approaches you, back away, even if you have to go around the corner to where you started.

If you can back up no farther, use your fierce attack while you circle around him and get into a position where you can back up again.

It won't take long for the Berzerker to drop him.

GIMLI

With Gimli, use the direct approach. Charge the Berzerker and repeatedly hit him with your fierce attack. When your skill meter is charged, back up using the jump, wait until he misses, then strike.

BATTLE 3

Two Orcs fly in front of you unconscious. A huge forest troll threw them; be careful.

ARAGORN

You face a large forest troll with a deadly mace. He seems like a daunting foe, but if you're careful, you can take him out.

Lure him into attacking you, then counterattack. To do this, stand at a distance until he throws a log at you. Don't worry if you miss the parry, the logs don't do much damage.

After he throws the log, make two fierce attacks, and stop close to him.

When he pulls back to hit you with his mace, hit L2 to jump out of reach.

When he misses, counterattack with another Double Hack ▲, ▲, then dodge and attack.

It takes many hits to fell this beast, but you can do it if you dodge and counterattack. Don't take too much damage.

LEGOLAS

Legolas follows a strategy similar to Aragorn's for taking down the forest troll. However, Legolas should use a single fierce attack, then run to safety rather than jump away.

GIMLI

Gimli uses the same strategy as Aragorn: fierce double attack, dodge, and then counterattack. This is an effective strategy for the Dwarf.

BATTLE 4

Next you run across an Orc camp. But the Orcs are preoccupied with something.

ARAGORN

Sneak up to the Orcs while their backs are turned. When they spot you, take out the four shields.

When the shields are gone, back up toward where you started this battle and make your stand. Attack combos, such as Isildur's Gambit (✕, ▲, ✕, ✕), allow you to string together perfect kill ratings.

Watch out for the Orcs with the double blades. They can work through your defenses.

LEGOLAS

Legolas can start this conflict with a few quick arrows, but you'll still have to deal with the shields.

Annihilate the shields, back up, then eliminate everyone from a distance with your arrows, or up close with your swords.

LEVEL 6: FANGORN FOREST

GIMLI

Take out the shields, then wipe out the Orcs. Parry the double blades.

Two Orcs jump out at you. Take them down, then eliminate the other attacking Orcs. Be on your guard until you hear the deep voice in the background signaling you've gotten them all.

TREASURE CHEST!

Next to one of the Orc tents lies a treasure chest. Bust it open and grab the health power-up inside.

TIP

Unless you see a kill rating, your target isn't dead. Orcs may fall under the water stunned, only to pop up moments later. Follow each knockdown with a fierce attack to slay these Orcs while they're on the ground.

Move forward until you see a waterfall. Go through the waterfall to progress to the next battle.

BATTLE 5

Walk into the river to continue. Be wary, though; it's full of deadly Orcs.

LEGOLAS

Follow Aragorn's strategy, but use your arrows at the first part of the battle to pick off the archers.

ARAGORN

When you hit the water, an Orc with a shield and two archers attack you on your right. First get the shield, then finish off the archers.

GIMLI

Gimli doesn't move well through the water, so be careful in these river battles. Make sure your enemies are dead so they don't pop up behind you.

Move upriver until you hit a point where the water swirls.

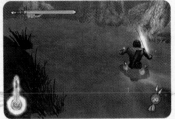

BATTLE 6

As you enter a cave, bats fly toward you, fearful of something bigger.

A forest troll busts through the cave wall ahead of you.

ARAGORN

Use a double fierce attack to take him out, jumping out of the way of his blow, then counterattack with two swipes of your blade. Repeat this until he dies.

TREASURE CHEST!

The cave that he busted out of holds a treasure chest. Open it and pick up an Elf-stone for extra experience.

Use your blade to break down the wooden barrier that was behind you and continue through the level.

LEGOLAS

Use the same technique that you used to slay the last forest troll—strike with a fierce attack and run away when he counters.

GIMLI

Follow Aragorn's strategy against this forest troll.

BATTLE 7

Use your sword to hack down the vines in your way; another Berzerker tries to block your path.

For all three characters, use the same strategy you used on the previous Berzerker. This one goes down the same way.

BATTLE 8

When you turn the next corner, you encounter a small group of Orcs. Some have the deadly double blades.

ARAGORN

Take these guys out, then finish off the archer who's barricaded farther down the path.

Around the next corner, a group of Goblins drops in on you from above. They are neither shielded nor dangerous, and you can get high kill ratings by slaying them together.

LEGOLAS

Use arrows on the Orcs that drop from above to build your skills and experience points.

GIMLI

Wade into the battles and wipe out the Orcs. Use combos to boost your kill ratings.

BATTLE 9

After you cut through another downed log, you see two forest trolls destroy some Orcs. When the action restarts, the forest trolls and two logs block the left path.

ARAGORN

Take the right path instead, after you chop down the vines blocking your way.

TREASURE CHEST!

Past the vines is a treasure chest containing a green health vial. If you don't need it now, don't open the chest—save it for later.

You now face two forest trolls at once. Concentrate on the first forest troll using past kill techniques. Don't worry about the other one; trolls rarely use teamwork.

TIP

Use your Rising Attack when a forest troll knocks you down. Hit ✕ to make a devastating strike on your way up.

When the first one is dead, take on the second. If you need health, go to the treasure chest you passed, open it, and grab the green health vial.

Vanquish the second forest troll using the familiar technique. You're done fighting in this level.

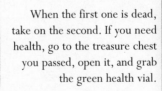

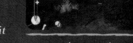

TREASURE CHEST!

Behind the forest trolls sits another treasure chest. Open it and grab the Elf-stone to add to your experience points.

Continue down the path, cut away the vines, and you're at the level's end!

LEGOLAS

Use your forest troll-killing techniques on these guys, one at a time.

GIMLI

Follow the same path and strategy as Aragorn.

SKILL UPGRADES

Your next mission requires you to fight heavily armed Uruk-hai. Prepare yourself with better defense and stronger combos.

ARAGORN

Purchase: Goblin Bane, Isildur's Deliverance
Cost: 4,000, 5,000
Use: Hit ■, ✕, R2 to instantly kill a goblin. Hit ▲, ✕, ✕, ▲ to take down shielded enemies with Isildur's Deliverance.
Reason: Goblin Bane is useful in Orthanc. Isildur's Deliverance is a deadly combo that builds skill points and dispatches shields.
Note: If you are not at level six, get the other required power-ups, pick one that you will use, and save experience points for later.

LEGOLAS

Purchase: Goblin Bane, Elrond's Gambit
Cost: 4,000, 5,000
Use: Hit ■, ✕, R2 to instantly kill a goblin. Hit ✕, ▲, ✕, ✕ to strike a couple of unshielded foes.
Reason: Goblin Bane is useful in Orthanc. Elrond's Gambit builds huge skill points.

GIMLI

Purchase: Goblin Bane, Might of Iron
Cost: 4,000, 10,000
Use: Hit ■, ✕, R2 to instantly kill a goblin. Might of Iron permanently adds to your life.
Reason: Goblin Bane is useful in Orthanc. Purchase Might of Iron to build Gimli into a powerful fighting force.

LEVEL 7: PLAINS OF ROHAN

GOALS
- PROTECT THE VILLAGERS
- DEFEAT THE URUK-HAI

PLAYABLE CHARACTERS

ARAGORN   LEGOLAS   GIMLI

LEGEND
- ⊛ BARREL (ELF-STONE)
- ▥ TREASURE CHEST (ELF-STONE)
- ● VILLAGERS TO BE RESCUED

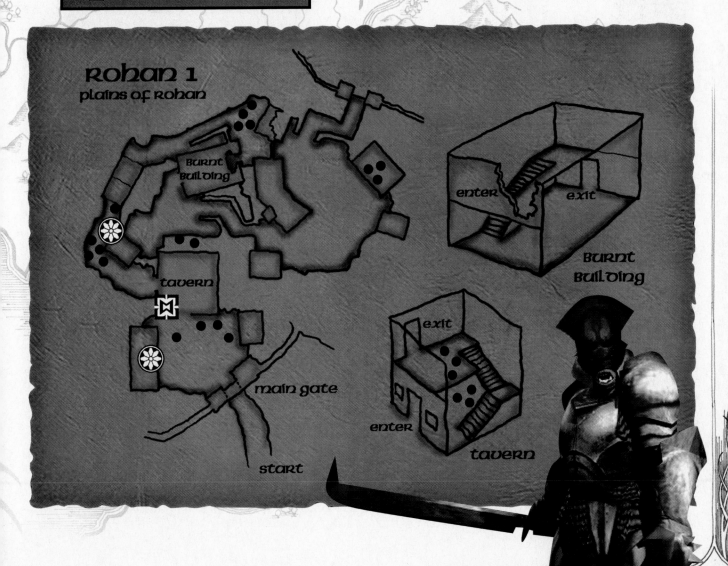

ROHAN 1
PLAINS OF ROHAN

BURNT BUILDING

enter   exit

BURNT BUILDING

tavern

exit

enter

tavern

main gate

start

ENEMIES

URUK-HAI   URUK-HAI CROSSBOWMAN   BERZERKER

WALKTHROUGH

The Uruk-hai are razing a village. You must stop them and save the villagers. It won't be easy.

NOTE

Strategies for this section work for all three characters unless otherwise noted.

CRUCIAL BATTLE INFORMATION

A new meter pops up on the upper-right side of your screen. This is your village health meter. Every time an uruk-hai kills a villager, the meter drops. when it gets to zero, you fail the mission.

You start at the village's main gate. Two Uruk-hai warriors attack you outside the gate; take them down.

Several more Uruk-hai are inside the courtyard; go after them before they hurt civilians.

Use your best combos to build up skill points, then take down the Uruk-hai whom Gandalf has wounded.

When all the Uruk-hai in the area are dead, Gandalf opens the door to the tavern and disappears. You'll run across him again soon.

ELF-STONE!

Before going inside the tavern, strike the barrels on the courtyard's left side. Inside one of them is an Elf-stone.

Head inside the tavern; a wall of fire has trapped several villagers.

Strike the barrel where the stairs and the flames meet to release the water inside. The water douses the flames, freeing the villagers.

Head upstairs and out the door. Move away from the door until you see a small barn. Several villagers run by. Go around the corner to face several bad guys.

After you free the villagers, a cutscene shows an Uruk-hai throw a villager from the upper story of the tavern onto flaming debris below.

If you made it here quickly enough, you'll see a Berzerker standing next to a fire. Attack him with your fierce attack or shove him with ●. He'll parry the attack, but you can push him into the fire. Then he is easy to kill.

When the villager crashes to the ground, another Uruk-hai comes through the tavern's door. Defeat him quickly.

There is also a barrel beside the fire. Hit it with your sword or shoot it with an arrow to release the water, douse the flames, and release the villager.

Climb the stairs and use your speed attack to destroy the three tables blocking the top of the stairs. This releases the three villagers upstairs.

Use arrows or speed attacks to dispatch the two crossbowmen, then head over the burning roof.

Don't hit them as they pass you down the stairs. Kill the two Uruk-hai in the room with you. Take out the Uruk-hai crossbowman from inside the room.

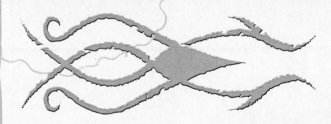

Continue until you see burning debris blocking an upward path. Shoot the barrel behind the debris to douse the flames.

When you exit, you see Gandalf fighting alone against a horde of Uruk-hai. Help him, but stay along the back side across from the door you left.

When the flames are gone, strike the debris across the path with a powerful blow. A combo such as ✗,✗,▲ works well.

Two more Uruk-hai are at the top of the path. End the encounter quickly.

After a few moments of fighting, a Berzerker comes through a door above and in front of you. He attacks the villagers.

A villager runs out of a burning building. You can't save him, and his death won't affect your villager health meter.

Use your arrows to shoot the Berzerker from below. It takes a couple of shots. Be careful; you may be attacked by an Uruk-hai, and you'll have to watch both fronts.

Enter the building he exited, and make a U-turn down the stairs to your left (when you enter). An Uruk-hai attacks you from downstairs. Hit him, and finish him with R2 while he's down.

LEGOLAS STRATEGY

If you're playing as Legolas, fight through this courtyard with your arrows. That way you're ready for the Berzerker when he steps out of the upstairs door.

Head downstairs, past another U-turn, to encounter another Uruk-hai who busts through the downstairs door of the burnt building.

LEVEL 7: PLAINS OF ROHAN

After you kill the Uruk-hai and the Berzerker, use your sword to take out the debris blocking the path out of the courtyard.

When you reach the top of the courtyard, a cutscene shows a battle between Uruk-hai and Rohan warriors.

LEGOLAS STRATEGY

As Legolas, you don't have to enter the upper courtyard to do battle. Instead, fire arrows into the battle to kill the uruk-hai. Watch the villager meter so they don't die in the fire.

After you protect the villagers and kill the Uruk-hai in the last area, move to the next level.

SKILL UPGRADES

Your characters may be able to use level six skills at this point. The next level requires a lot of ranged attacks, so upgrade in this area.

ARAGORN

Purchase: Master Swordsman
Cost: 10,000
Use: This automatically increases the damage of your speed attack.
Reason: In future battles, you will need to kill many foes. A boosted speed attack helps do this.

LEGOLAS

Purchase: Dragonfire Arrows, Elrond's Deliverance
Cost: 8,000, 5,000
Use: The Dragonfire Arrows set fire to their targets. Hit ▲,✕,✕,▲ to take out shielded enemies with Elrond's Deliverance.
Reason: The Dragonfire Arrows are deadly and can kill almost any unarmored foe in a short time. Elrond's Deliverance is a major skill meter builder.

GIMLI

Purchase: Balin's Gambit, Moria Axes
Cost: 5,000, 4,000
Use: Hit ✕,▲,✕,✕ to take out multiple foes with Balin's Gambit. The Moria Axes increase the damage of your ranged attack.
Reason: Ranged attacks are Gimli's weakest area. Boost it with Moria Axes, and add new combos, like Balin's Gambit.

CRUCIAL BATTLE INFORMATION

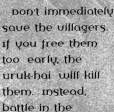

The uruk-hai capture villagers in a building. A new meter pops up below the villagers' health meter. Save these villagers before the new meter drops to zero.

Don't immediately save the villagers. If you free them too early, the uruk-hai will kill them. Instead, battle in the courtyard, killing the bad guys while keeping a close eye on the smaller villager health meter.

When the meter gets close to bottoming out, bust through the debris, release the prisoners, and protect them against any remaining uruk-hai.

LEVEL 8: THE WESTFOLD

GOALS
- SLAY YOUR ENEMIES
- DESTROY THE EXPLOSIVES

PLAYABLE CHARACTERS

ARAGORN LEGOLAS GIMLI

LEGEND

1	Battle 1		6	Battle 6
2	Battle 2		7	Battle 7
3	Battle 3		✲	Treasure chest (Elf-stone)
4	Battle 4		⊞	Barrel (health)
5	Battle 5			

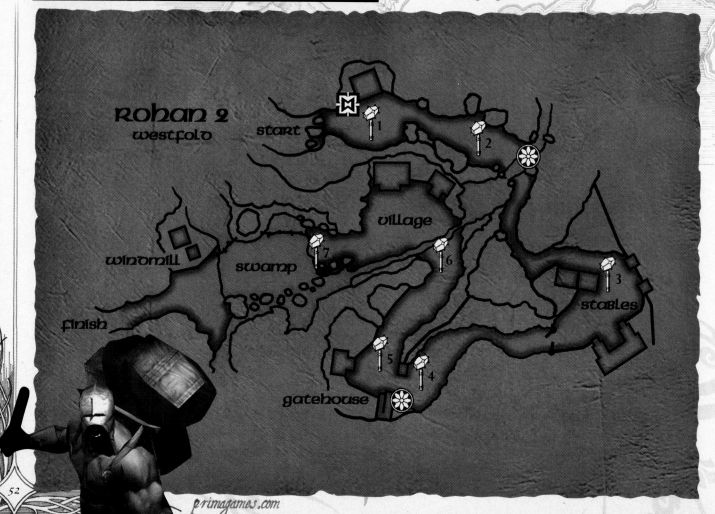

Rohan 2
westfold   start

windmill   swamp

finish

village

gatehouse

stables

Enemies

BERZERKER

URUK-HAI BOMBER

URUK-HAI CROSSBOWMAN

URUK-HAI MELEE

ORC MELEE

ORC WITH SHIELD

URUK-HAI SCOUT

Saruman's forces are moving massive amounts of explosives through the Westfold. You must stop them.

Walkthrough

In this mission, you can easily make it through if you use the explosives strewn across the map. This strategy will get you through, but you won't gather as much experience. Because of this, we break down each encounter into two paths: the easy path and the experience path.

TIP
If you want later levels to be easier, take the experience path, otherwise you'll come out of this mission without many experience points.

Battle 1

You begin in a small village. There are carts of explosives everywhere, so be careful.

THE EASY PATH
Stand back in your starting position, and start using your ranged attack weapon. It will automatically lock on to the explosive carts and blow them up.

Let the enemies come close to the carts so you can take them out in groups. Once you've blown up all the carts, move on.

THE EXPERIENCE PATH
When the action starts, move to your left and forward to stay away from the explosive carts. Then start cautiously fighting the approaching bad guys.

Be extremely careful, because if you combo a move you may end up striking farther than you expected and hitting one of the carts. This will damage you and most likely steal your kill and experience points.

TIP
Be careful using your ranged attacks in this level. Your weapon usually locks on to an explosive target first. If you're trying to avoid blowing everything up, stick to your melee weapon.

BATTLE 2

THE EASY PATH

In the next open area, several enemies cluster around another explosive cart. Wait until they approach, then shoot the cart with your ranged weapon. This should take out most of the bad guys.

Shoot the next cart to take out the crossbowman in the back of the area and you've got this small section cleared.

THE EXPERIENCE PATH

Shoot the first explosive cart right away. Or, avoid it altogether and let the bad guys come to you.

Take out the bad guys when they get close and then charge the crossbowman in the back to finish him off. Watch out for the cart behind him.

TREASURE CHEST!

In the creek running behind this small area lies a treasure chest with an Elf-stone inside. You'll need this, whichever approach you take.

When you open the treasure chest, two more Orcs crop up. Take them both out quickly. Use combos to gain more experience. Before you reach the corner you'll battle an Orc with a shield.

LEVEL 8: THE WESTFOLD

BATTLE 3

THE EASY PATH

When you turn the corner you'll see three Uruk-hai bombers carrying explosives. Quickly fire a ranged attack to annihilate them in a chain reaction.

Run down to the bottom of the stables and shoot a ranged attack at the explosive carts around the outside of the stable area.

There are still some bad guys left to attack you, and behind them more Uruk-hai bombers are on their way. Wait until the mad bombers are close, then take them out with a ranged attack. They will kill many of their fellow bad guys.

THE EXPERIENCE PATH

Kill the first Uruk-hai bomber that comes up the hill toward you and quickly shoot at the third one in the line. If you're swift, you'll kill the last one before he dies in the chain reaction of explosives.

Run down to the stables and immediately jump into the fray. Get as many kills as possible before the Uruk-hai bombers approach.

When one does approach, immediately use your ranged attack from a distance. Kill him without eliminating the guys you're trying to get experience points from.

Stay in the back corner of the stables and shoot your ranged attack at a seemingly endless supply of Uruk-hai bombers. You won't get many experience points for each, but eventually they do add up.

BATTLE 4

THE EASY PATH

After a brief cutscene, you're attacked by an Orc with a shield. Defeat him and move down into the gatehouse area.

You see a cart with explosives. Wait until the enemy approaches it and hit it with your ranged attack.

Hit the rest of the explosive carts in the gatehouse area with your ranged attack to eliminate nearly everyone.

THE EXPERIENCE PATH

Hit the first cart immediately and you won't kill any enemies.

Stand in the spot where the cart was found and make your stand. You should eliminate quite a few bad guys. Try to use combos. This is a good opportunity to score some perfect kills.

Once the remaining enemies are dead, pick off the other explosive carts from a distance.

TREASURE CHEST!

As you pass through the gatehouse area, you'll see a treasure chest inside a burning building. It holds an Elf-stone.

Don't try to step in and grab it. Instead, go around the far side of the building, climb the stairs, and look for two barrels at the top of the second flight of steps.

Use your ranged attack to shoot one of the barrels and release the water down on the burning steps.

Climb the steps and use your speed attack to smash one of the barrels; the water will douse the flames below.

Go back downstairs and open the treasure chest inside the room without getting burned. Grab the Elf-stone.

Level 8: The Westfold

BATTLE 5

Once you head back downstairs, you encounter more enemies. Get ready for a quick fight.

THE EASY PATH

Back up quickly and start firing ranged attacks. Very soon, some Uruk-hai bombers will run toward you.

Hit one of them to blow up everyone in the area with a massive chain reaction.

THE EXPERIENCE PATH

Rush to take out the nearby attackers as quickly as possible. You should be able to get a kill or two before the bomber approaches.

Eventually you must start the chain reaction. If you stay near the bottom of the stairs, you can range attack a near endless supply of suicide attackers.

BATTLE 6

You approach a small village on the other side of a creek. Be careful once again; there are explosives everywhere.

THE EASY PATH

Just hang back and attack with ranged weapons. You'll set off explosives and the enemies will often be hit by the flames from their own bombers.

Stay back until you need to finish off the surviving enemies.

LEGOLAS STRATEGY

Aim carefully to take out many enemies with your arrows while you stand safely on the other side of the creek.

THE EXPERIENCE PATH

Run across the creek, attack the enemy, and return to where you started. Your enemies will follow, and you can take them down safely away from the explosives.

BATTLE 7

Use your melee weapon to take out the debris lying across your path toward the windmill. As you approach, you must eliminate a couple of enemies.

Neither path is exceptionally simple at this stage. You need to wade across the water to fight the troops on the other side.

Three enemies are hiding under the water, so be wary, but always keep an eye out for the Uruk-hai bombers. They will be constantly running toward you.

THE EASY PATH

Once you get past the underwater enemies, start making ranged attacks toward the bad guys on the other shore. Hit the bombers as soon as they appear and you'll take out some more enemies with the blast.

THE EXPERIENCE PATH

You can also slog your way across to the other shore and fight them on land. This is difficult and risky.

Finally, fire a ranged attack at one of the explosive carts beneath the windmill to send the entire place up in smoke and end the level.

SKILL UPGRADES

Your next mission will be a short fight against a boss. Pick items that will help you for the following level.

ARAGORN

Purchase: Orc Bane, Gondor Bow
Cost: 6,000, 6,000
Use: Hit ■, ✕, R2 to take out an Orc with a single blow using Orc Bane. The Gondor Bow is the best ranged weapon that Aragorn can use.
Reason: The Orc Bane and Gondor Bow will be useful two levels from now, but there's no sense in waiting to purchase them.

LEGOLAS

Purchase: Orc Bane, Mithril Arrows
Cost: 6,000, 10,000
Use: Hit ■, ✕, R2 to kill an Orc with a single blow using Orc Bane. The Mithril Arrows penetrate and damage all enemies in their path *and* light them on fire.
Reason: You'll need both of these later. Just remember that you still need one more ranged weapon upgrade.

GIMLI

Purchase: Orc Bane, Mountain Rage
Cost: 6,000, 4,000
Use: Hit ■, ✕, R2 to eliminate an Orc with a single blow using Orc Bane. Mountain Rage gives you a more deadly charged fierce attack.
Reason: You'll need these both soon enough.

LEVEL 9: GAP OF ROHAN

GOAL
- SLAY THE WARGS AND RIDERS

PLAYABLE CHARACTERS

ARAGORN   LEGOLAS   GIMLI

LEGEND
- ❀ BARREL (ELF-STONE)
- ✸ BOSS BATTLE STARTING POINT

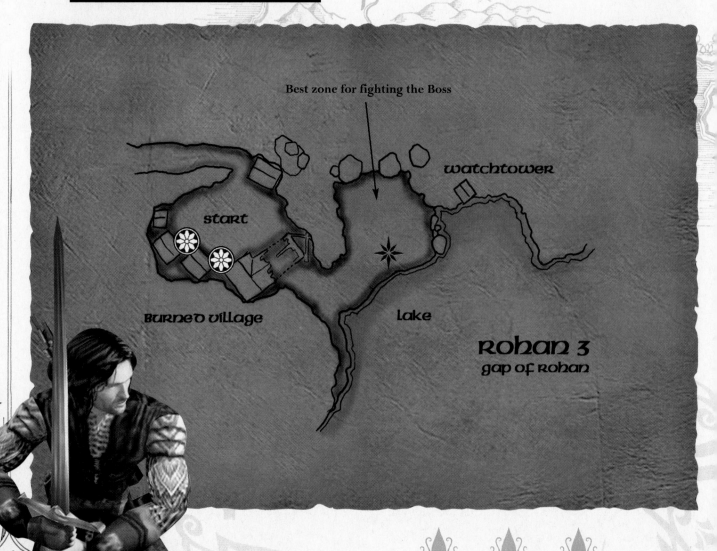

Best zone for fighting the Boss

WATCHTOWER

START

BURNED VILLAGE

LAKE

ROHAN 3
GAP OF ROHAN

Enemies

WARG RIDER

WARG

Walkthrough

The Gap of Rohan is a short but difficult level—if you don't know the trick to completing it. If you do, you'll pass through in minutes.

Battle 1

You start in a small burned village, under attack from two Wargs and Orc riders. Strike with your ranged attack. Your partners attack as well, so be the one who administers the kill to get the experience points.

It won't take long for the Wargs and their riders to die.

When they're down, pick up nearby power-ups. There are a couple of green health vials close at hand. Grab them if you need them.

When you grab the experience power-ups, break through the debris blocking your path out of the village.

After you do this, the building collapses, blocking you from your fellow travelers. You have to go this one alone.

You end up in a big field, joined by a group of Warg Riders.

After the cutscene plays, two rush you. Quickly parry.

They return to their starting positions. Take them out with your ranged attack.

Level 9: Gap of Rohan

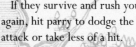
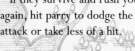
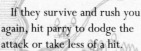

If they survive and rush you again, hit parry to dodge the attack or take less of a hit.

Parry to protect yourself when his Warg charges.

Eventually you will eliminate all except the center one. He's the toughest, and he can block all your arrows.

When he returns to his base position, he will do one of three things: charge again, call in another Warg, or hold onto his Warg as it rises on its hind legs.

CRUCIAL BATTLE INFORMATION

When you reach the point where there is only the Sharkû left, his health meter shows in the upperright corner of your screen.

If he charges again, parry again and wait for him to return. Even if you get knocked down, you won't take much damage if you parry. Don't worry about him attacking you from the rear. He rarely does that.

If he calls in another Warg and rider, back up to the middle of the field and get your ranged weapon ready. Repeatedly fire your ranged weapon when the second Warg is set on the same field you are.

Approach the far side of the field you are fighting in and stay a couple of safe yards from this boss.

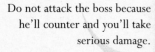

Do not attack the boss because he'll counter and you'll take serious damage.

Level 9: Gap of Rohan

If he holds onto his Warg while it rises on its hind legs, use that time to make your attack.

ISILDUR'S SWIFT TERROR

Don't try too many shots at a time. If you know how to parry his charges and how to take down any other Warg Riders, you can whittle him down and pick up extra experience points.

Repeat the pattern of parry, wait, and attack when the Warg is on its hind feet. Before long, this boss will be dead and the level will be done.

You should gain an experience level by the time you finish this mission. You'll need it; things get more difficult from here on out.

SKILL UPGRADES

You are about to step up to a new level of challenge, testing your melee skills. Max out whatever skills you can to be prepared.

ARAGORN

Purchase: Bane of Saruman
Cost: 8,000
Use: Hit ■,✕,R2 to instantly kill an Uruk-hai.
Reason: After you have the Orc Bane, the Goblin Bane, and the Bane of Saruman, you can take out any attacker with an instant combo.
Note: Save your extra experience for the next level.

LEGOLAS

Purchase: Bane of Saruman
Cost: 8,000
Use: Hit ■,✕,R2 to instantly kill an Uruk-hai.
Reason: After you have the Orc Bane, the Goblin Bane, and the Bane of Saruman, you can kill any attacker with an instant combo.
Note: Save your extra experience for the next level.

GIMLI

Purchase: Bane of Saruman
Cost: 8,000
Use: Hit ■,✕,R2 to instantly kill an Uruk-hai.
Reason: After you have the Orc Bane, the Goblin Bane, and the Bane of Saruman, you can take out any attacker with an instant combo.
Note: Save your extra experience for the next level.

LEVEL 9: GAP OF ROHAN

LEVEL 10-HELM'S DEEP: THE DEEPING WALL

GOAL

- PROTECT THE DEEPING WALL FROM BEING OVERRUN BY SARUMAN'S FORCES.

PLAYABLE CHARACTERS

ARAGORN   LEGOLAS   GIMLI

LEGEND

- ✷ Barrel (Elf-stone)
- ⊡ Treasure chest (health)
- ● Ladder position

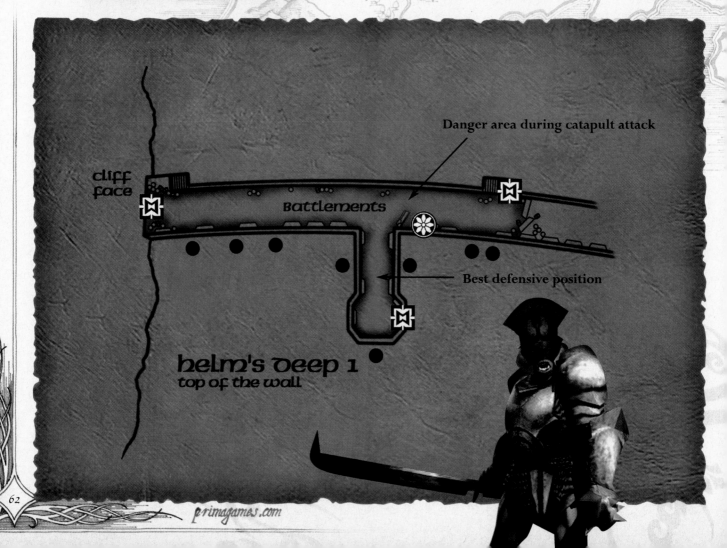

Danger area during catapult attack

cliff face

Battlements

Best defensive position

helm's deep 1
top of the wall

ENEMIES

GOBLIN   **GOBLIN WITH SHIELD**   **ORC WITH SHIELD**

ORC MELEE   **BERZERKER**   **URUK-HAI MELEE**

WALKTHROUGH

This level tests your close-quarters combat skills as you fight off a legion of Saruman's forces trying to overtake the wall into Helm's Deep.

The opening cutscene shows Legolas and Gimli kick over some ladders. This should give you an idea about how you can beat this level.

CRUCIAL BATTLE INFORMATION

A new meter displayed on the upper right corner of your screen shows an overview of the fighting area with red markers showing where ladders are leaning against the wall.

A meter inside this diagram fills when enemy forces are on the wall. As more bad guys join you on the wall, the gauge rises. If it fills and flashes for a few seconds, you have failed your mission.

You begin near the ladder on the right side of the wall. Kick it using ●.

Run to the part of the wall that points toward the enemy forces; kick down the ladder at the far end.

The section of the wall that juts out from the rest of the wall is the best place to make your defensive stand because you have three ladder positions close together, all visible on a single screen.

Head toward the left side of the wall. You can avoid this area for the rest of the level, but there's something you need to grab.

ELF-STONE!

Destroy the barrels at the map's lower-left corner where the wall juts out. Inside one of them is an Elf-stone. Grab it.

Kick down the ladder or ladders on that side and return to the middle section of the map, killing any enemies in your way.

STEP-BY-STEP GUIDE

At this point you should begin the strategy that will take you through the end of this level. It's a basic nine-step process.

STEP 1: CHECK THE ENEMY METER

If the meter on your screen's upper-right side is red, kill the nearest bad guys. After the meter drops, move to step 2.

STEP 2: TAKE DOWN ANY LADDERS IN THE MIDDLE AREA

Check your main defensive area. Look on the meter on your screen or make a visual check. If any ladders are leaning against the middle section of the wall kick them down with ●.

STEP 3: KILL ANY BAD GUYS IN THE MIDDLE AREA

Clear the entire section of the wall that juts out. Annihilate every foe in the area.

STEP 4: CHECK FOR NEW LADDERS

If any new ladders came up while you were fighting, kick them down. If not, continue to Step 5.

STEP 5: TAKE DOWN THE LADDERS ON THE WALL'S RIGHT SIDE

Run along the wall and knock down all three ladders in that section. You may have to fight to make a path to all three.

STEP 7: FIGHT ENEMIES IN THE RIGHT-HAND SECTION

Use combo moves to build experience. If you only kick down ladders, you won't have many experience points to use.

STEP 8: RETURN TO THE MIDDLE WHEN NEW LADDERS APPEAR

Keep an eye on your enemy meter, and when you see a red marker go up in the middle section, go to the middle.

Level 10—Helm's Deep: The Deeping Wall

STEP 9: RETURN TO STEP 1

Throughout this process, watch your enemy meter. When it hits red, go to Step 1 and kill a couple of bad guys.

WAVE 1

During the battle, there are several waves of attacks. The first wave is straightforward. After you hold off the enemy for a while, they fire flaming arrows at you.

WAVE 2

Stay close to the battlements and keep your eyes out for incoming arrows. These arrows are a minor distraction. They won't hurt you much, and even if they do, the attacking enemies drop health power-ups.

You can also dodge the arrows if you see them coming in waves. Alternatively, position yourself so an enemy is between you and the arrows, and the arrows may do some of the work for you.

Pay attention when someone yells at you to "get down" or "take cover;" this means a dangerous group of arrows is coming in. Either parry or dodge these attacks.

WAVE 3

Another cutscene shows Saruman's forces using catapults. When this happens, adjust your strategy.

After the catapult fires, stay clear of the center of the wall. Stick close to the battlements as you run through your step-by-step pattern.

LEVEL 10—HELM'S DEEP: THE DEEPING WALL

Keep your eyes open. You can see when a catapult attack is on its way. Although it is tough to judge, you can guess where not to go.

The good news is that catapult attacks often take out some of Saruman's own troops. Don't go down with them.

During the third wave, Berzerkers get to the wall. Do not fight these warriors if you have trouble beating them. Avoid them, take out weaker troops, and knock down ladders.

You won't have to suffer the last wave long. Reinforcements arrive, and you will have cleared the level.

SKILL UPGRADES

Your next mission demands that you use your ranged attacks. Build these up to their maximum.

ARAGORN

Purchase: Wilderness Rage, Wrath of Númenor
Cost: 4,000, 6,000
Use: Hold down ▲ to charge your sword and release for a powerful Wrath of Númenor attack that sets ablaze anyone it hits.
Reason: This is a useful skill for taking out large groups of enemies and trolls with a single blow.

LEGOLAS

Purchase: Elven Bow Mastery
Cost: 10,000
Use: This skill increases the damage of each arrow attack.
Reason: You can beat the next level by ranged weapons if you upgrade your arrows and your archery skills.
Note: Make sure you have the Mithril Arrows upgrade before you purchase this skill. They are more important, but both together are best.

GIMLI

Purchase: Misty Mountain Axes, Mountain Rage
Cost: 6,000, 4,000
Use: The Misty Mountain Axes automatically make your ranged attacks more powerful. Hold down ▲ to charge your axe, then release for a powerful Mountain Rage attack.
Reason: Both of these skills will make the next level easier for you.

LEVEL 11—HELM'S DEEP: THE BREACHED WALL

GOALS

- PROTECT THE GATE LEADING INTO HELM'S DEEP
- DESTROY THE CATAPULT

PLAYABLE CHARACTERS

ARAGORN   LEGOLAS   GIMLI

LEGEND

⚙ catapult location

hole in deeping wall

Best position for fighting the cave-troll

helm's deep 2
the breached wall

Best defensive position

start

gate

ENEMIES

ORC MELEE   BERZERKER   URUK-HAI MELEE

URUK-HAI BOMBER   URUK-HAI CROSSBOWMAN   ORC WITH SHIELD

ORC ARCHER   CAVE-TROLL

WALKTHROUGH

This level is incredibly difficult. The enemies come in waves. Your skill with ranged attacks will be tested, as will your ability to think clearly in the midst of chaos.

No strategy makes this level easy, but if you know what enemies are in each wave, you can prepare to take them out.

CRUCIAL BATTLE INFORMATION

The level starts with a meter on your screen representing the remaining integrity of the gate. If it drops to nothing, the enemy has breached the gate, and you have failed.

WAVE 1

The first group of enemies is a line of Uruk-hai bombers. Enjoy this break; this is as easy as things get.

Use your ranged attack to pick them off. Don't attack too quickly, though. You want some to approach at least midway, so you can reload with the ranged ammo they drop.

WAVE 2

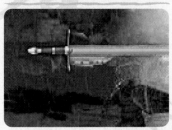

A bomber runs ahead of a group of shielded Orcs. Wait until they are all together and hit the bomber with a ranged attack.

WAVE 3

Another group of Orcs runs with another bomber. Use the same technique. If you miss either of these bombers, you'll have to take on the Orcs with your sword.

WAVE 4

Another group of Orcs follows another bomber. Use timing to hit the bomber when he's alongside the Orcs so you don't have to fight them one at a time.

Chase down those you didn't kill and keep an eye out for bombers that follow them.

> ### TIP
> *If you have to fight Orcs near the gate, step away from the gate and attack from behind or from the side while they're distracted by their demolition work.*

WAVE 8

You face a mixed group of shielded and unshielded Orcs. Use your charged attack or individually take them out. Watch for the bombers behind them.

WAVE 5

Another group is coming. Use the same technique. Finish off the ones you missed with your sword.

LEGOLAS STRATEGY

If you purchase the **MITHRIL** arrows, you have a huge advantage playing through this level as Legolas. Not only is the impact of these arrows deadly, but they also light their targets on fire.

When playing as Legolas, stand near the gate and take out any unshielded enemies (except the troll). Use this strategy to eliminate foes from a distance.

WAVE 6

A huge pack of unshielded Orcs arrives. Destroy as many as you can with ranged attacks, then kill the rest with your sword.

This group is followed by a near-continuous stream of bombers. Shoot them from a distance. They can do more damage to the gate than even a large group of Orcs.

Some enemies, like Berzerkers, take longer to fall. After they're on fire, let them burn, then focus on someone else.

WAVE 7

Shielded Orcs attack. If you purchased a charged-up fierce attack, build up your attack as they approach and unleash it when the Orcs are in range.

WAVE 9

This wave is intense. It starts with a mix of Uruk-hai and Orcs. Hit the Uruk-hai, then turn to the Orcs.

Following them is a ton of bombers and more Orcs. Keep these guys at a distance with your ranged attack. Set off chain reactions that kill many enemies in a single blow.

WAVE 10

As if that last wave wasn't difficult enough, a wave of several Uruk-hai and a Berzerker follow it.

Weaken the Berzerker with ranged attacks before he gets to you, then focus on the Uruk-hai. Get rid of the Berzerker while he's concentrating on the gate.

Before you finish this wave, a cutscene shows a line of crossbowmen that aims to make your life difficult.

WAVE 11

With the crossbowmen at his back, a Berzerker starts the next wave. Use ranged attacks to weaken him, then put him out of commission.

An Uruk-hai and some more bombers follow the Berzerker. Hit the bombers while they are near the crossbowmen to kill some of those arrow launchers.

Another cutscene plays. Things are about to get worse.

WAVE 12

You face a couple more bombers. Shoot them and use your ranged attack to bombard the crossbowmen.

WAVE 13

Now things get tough. This wave starts with a huge cave-troll and a stream of bombers behind him.

You may also have crossbowmen still in your way. Run past the cave-troll to take them out first.

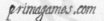

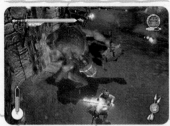

After the crossbowmen are down, use the field to your advantage. If you stay by the gate, the troll may get between you and the bombers and allow them to approach too close to the gate.

The bombers demand the majority of your attention. You can slowly weaken the troll by attacking with your fierce attack, then using L2 to dodge.

It's more important to take out the bombers. After you clear the area of bombers with your ranged attack, attack at the cave-troll.

Don't try to get two attacks in a row. Instead, clear the area of bombers, then return for a single attack against the troll. Repeat this until you kill him.

Another cutscene shows the catapult rolling onto the field in front of you. It is flanked by a large number of Orc and Uruk-hai warriors.

WAVE 14

The Uruk-hai leader rushes you. Use a charged fierce attack or fight him normally. He's not difficult to kill.

Charge the large group of troops. Don't kill them all before you approach the catapult. Make a run for the war machine.

Slice your way through the first wave of shielded Orcs. Take out crossbowmen who are close and watch out for exploding charges. If you're lucky, these will blow up some of the enemies instead of you.

CRUCIAL BATTLE INFORMATION

A new power meter shows up. It is the catapult's health meter. Attack the armor around the catapult until the meter reaches zero.

Run past the Uruk-hai and attack the catapult's corner. Stand in the spot between the front and side armor.

Fight any foes who follow you to this spot. The dead drop enough health to keep you going.

Keep an eye out for explosive charges from Uruk-hai cross-bowmen. You do not want to die after coming this far.

Hack away at the armor on both the side and front of the catapult.

When you are done, go to the other side of the catapult and destroy the armor there.

After the armor's gone, smash the catapult with the Devastating Attack. You've made it through this difficult level.

SKILL UPGRADES

The next level pits you against countless enemies in a huge battle. Purchase powerful combos or upgrade your health.

ARAGORN

Purchase: Isildur's Judgment, Strength of the Argonath
Cost: 5,000, 10,000
Use: Hit ▲, ▲, ●, ▲ to knock a shielded foe to the ground and strike him with Isildur's Judgment. The Strength of the Argonath will boost your health.
Reason: These are useful for the dangerous battle into which you're heading.

LEGOLAS

Purchase: Elrond's Judgment
Cost: 5,000
Use: Hit ▲, ▲, ●, ▲ to knock a shielded foe to the ground and strike him.
Reason: This is a useful attack for the conflict coming up.

GIMLI

Purchase: Axe Mastery of Kings, Balin's Judgement
Cost: 10,000, 5,000
Use: These boost the damage inflicted by your fierce attack.
Reason: You'll need all the damage you can dish out for the next level.

LEVEL 12-HELM'S DEEP: HORNBURG COURTYARD

GOALS
- PROTECT THE BARRICADE
- RESCUE LEGOLAS (OR ARAGORN)
- KILL THE ARCHERS

LEGEND
◈ ENEMY ARCHERS DURING STAGE 4

PLAYABLE CHARACTERS

ARAGORN   LEGOLAS   GIMLI

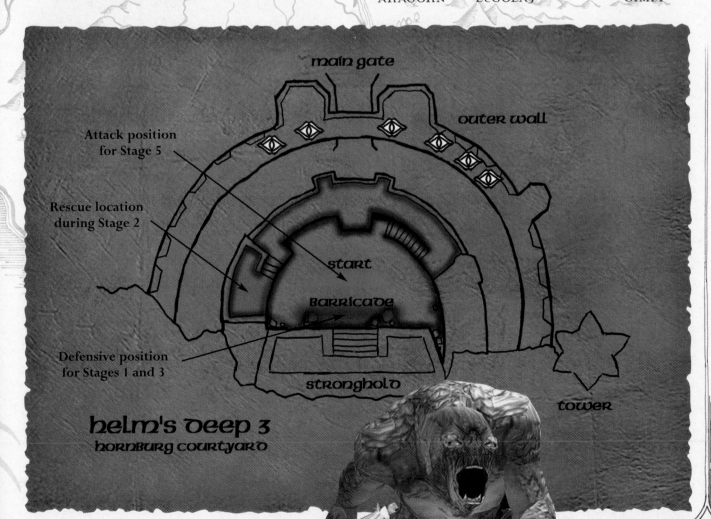

main gate

outer wall

Attack position for Stage 5

Rescue location during Stage 2

start

Barricade

Defensive position for Stages 1 and 3

stronghold

tower

helm's Deep 3
hornburg courtyard

THE LORD OF THE RINGS
THE TWO TOWERS

ENEMIES

GOBLIN WITH SHIELD · **ORC MELEE** · **BERZERKER**

URUK-HAI MELEE · **URUK-HAI CROSSBOWMAN** · **ORC WITH SHIELD**

ORC ARCHER · **CAVE-TROLL**

WALKTHROUGH

This is it. Everything you've learned and all the skills you've purchased with your hard-earned experience come down to this.

You face more enemies than you ever imagined possible, but if you've purchased the right skills and know how to use them, you'll emerge victorious from this difficult battle.

CRUCIAL BATTLE INFORMATION

The meter on your screen represents the remaining integrity of the barricade. You must keep it from zeroing out.

Saruman's forces have broken through the wall, and they're storming Hornburg Courtyard. Make a stand before the barricade falls.

STAGE 1

You begin in the middle of this fierce battle, so start swinging.

Use your combos to build your skill meter to its peak. With the number of targets, you can quickly do this.

You're looking for perfect kill ratings, not necessarily because you'll get more experience, but because you'll double the damage of your attacks when your skill meter is full.

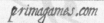

Take advantage of these moments when your skills are at their maximum and destroy as many enemies as you can before they drop.

Your main targets are any enemies beating on the barricade. Keep the barricade meter full to give yourself more time to ward off future attackers.

Move back and forth across the barricade's face, and kill anything that crosses your path. By protecting this area, you'll protect the barricade.

TIP

Don't worry about getting hit or knocked down. With so many enemies falling, you'll always find a health power-up nearby.

Don't get drawn away from the barricade by attackers. It doesn't help to fight in the middle of the courtyard if the enemy can walk up and attack the barricade.

LEGOLAS STRATEGY

If you've upgraded your arrows to their full extent, stand in a corner and fire—but only if you're playing as Legolas.

Target the enemies at the barricade. If you miss them, they pound on the doors.

No matter how good an archer you are, you'll have to fight hand-to-hand. Be prepared and use your best combos.

GIMLI STRATEGY

While playing as Gimli, use your charged fierce attack to clear out large groups of foes. Also, use your Rising Attack to get revenge when they knock you down.

Even in the midst of chaos, pay attention and use the right combos. If, for instance, you're next to an Orc with a shield, use Elrond's/Balin's/Isildur's Judgment (▲,▲,●,▲) to take him down.

STAGE 2

In the middle of the battle, one of your teammates (either Legolas or Aragorn, depending upon whom you're playing as) cries for help on the wall. Save him quickly.

You reach a short set of stairs and see your friend under attack from several Uruk-hai.

Jump into the battle and cut them down. Be wary of the one without a helmet; he is the most deadly.

CRUCIAL BATTLE INFORMATION

A temporary health meter shows up for either Aragorn or Legolas; rescue him before the meter runs out.

ELF-STONE!

One of the Uruk-hai drops an Elf-stone when he dies. Don't forget it; experience is always valuable.

Fight out of the traffic in front of the barricade. This is easier said than done, so focus on cutting through, not scoring kills.

LEGOLAS STRATEGY

Legolas can easily take care of all three Uruk-hai using his MITHRIL arrows. Fire as you go up the second set of stairs, then watch them burn.

When you get out of the mayhem, go to the stairs in the back of the courtyard. Watch out for enemies that chase you.

When you finish, your friend's health meter disappears. Return to the barricade.

Turn left when you reach the top of the stairs and run along the wall, ignoring enemies.

Don't run straight back, though. Instead, watch out for catapult attacks. If you just make a straight run, you'll be nailed by an explosion.

Stage 3

Your other friend fights near the barricade; he needs your help. Get down there.

There are even tougher foes now. Stick to your combos and you'll do fine.

Establish your defensive path along the wall to keep the enemy at bay and your skill meter at its peak.

As you fight, flaming arrows fly in. These can mess you up.

Stage 4

Soon afterward, someone calls out, "There are archers on the wall." When you hear this, leave the battle in the barricade and go upstairs.

Shoot the archers on the outer wall (see map). If you need to, clear a defensive path between the inner wall and the enemy beforehand.

Don't dawdle. Rapidly shoot the archers on the other wall. You must hit at least five. Shoot offscreen to the left until you no longer receive skill points for each shot.

When enough of the archers are dead, someone calls your character's name. Return to the barricade.

Berzerkers have been added to the mix, and they're tough. But you can handle them at this stage, thanks to your improved skills. If not, avoid them.

Fight to the barricade and establish your defensive zone once again.

Stage 5

Another cutscene plays and your worst nightmare occurs. Two trolls climb over the wall and join the fray.

Focus immediately on these trolls. Nothing else matters if you can't stop them.

To defeat them, use your charged attack when their backs are turned. Be careful, however; they can hit you with the backs of their maces.

Run behind them, charge up, and strike to take one down. You can also hit them with combos and, when they hit you, pick up nearby health.

If that doesn't work, draw the troll away from the barricade and use your past troll-killing technique: fierce attack, evade, then attack again.

When the first one dies, go after the second. When he dies, you've finished the level.

You've made it through a tough game. Now check out the special missions.

SKILL UPGRADES

You've finished the game— now you can test your skills in the special missions. Use any and all experience points to max out your health.

ARAGORN

Purchase: Strength of the Argonath
Cost: 10,000
Use: If you couldn't afford this earlier, buy it now. The Strength of the Argonath boosts your health.
Reason: Your next level requires all the health you've got. Make sure you have the Wrath of Númenor, too.

LEGOLAS

Purchase: Force of Galadriel
Cost: 10,000
Use: If you couldn't afford this earlier, buy it now. The Force of Galadriel boosts your health.
Reason: Your next level requires all the health you've got. Make sure you have the *Mithril* Arrows upgrade as well.

GIMLI

Purchase: Might of the Khazad-dûm
Cost: 10,000
Use: This is another health increase.
Reason: Now's the time to build up health. Make sure you have the Wrath of Moria first; it's important.

SECRET MISSION-ARAGORN

TOWER OF ORTHANC

GOAL
- SURVIVE 20 FLOORS OF THE TOWER OF ORTHANC

PLAYABLE CHARACTER

ARAGORN

WALKTHROUGH

FLOOR 1

URUK-HAI SCOUT X 5

Use Isildur's combos or try the Bane of Saruman (■, ✕, R2) to sweep these guys away.

FLOOR 2

URUK-HAI SCOUT X 2   ORC WITH SHIELD X 4

Either use your regular combos or run away from these guys, charge your fierce attack, then light them on fire.

IMPORTANT STRATEGY

start each floor by running away from the middle, charging your sword before the enemies appear, and attacking whoever's nearest to you. If you've purchased wrath of númenor, you'll light multiple foes on fire.

this takes out up to three of your foes before the action starts. use this strategy on every floor for best results.

Floor 3

URUK-HAI SCOUT X 2   **ORC MELEE X 4**

This combination is tough if you fight the bad guys up close. Get some distance and take them out a few at a time.

Floor 4

URUK-HAI SCOUT X 3   **ORC WITH SHIELD X 3**

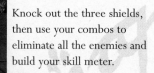

Knock out the three shields, then use your combos to eliminate all the enemies and build your skill meter.

Floor 5

ORC MELEE X 3   **ORC WITH SHIELD X 3**

Use Isildur's Judgment to kill the Orcs with shields. Other combos work on the regular Orcs.

Floor 6

ORC ARCHER X 8

Run and dodge around the outside of the circle, killing the archers one at a time. If you zigzag from archer to archer, you won't get hit often.

Floor 7

URUK-HAI SCOUT X 2   **ORC MELEE X 2**   **ORC ARCHER X 4**

Run, dodge, and focus on the four Orc archers first. When they're dead, combo through the rest.

Floor 8

ORC WITH SHIELD X 4

ORC ARCHER X 4

Take out the Orc archers first, but if the Orcs with shields hassle you, use Isildur's Judgment (▲, ▲, ●, ▲) to take them down.

Floor 9

ORC MELEE X 2   ORC WITH SHIELD X 2   ORC ARCHER X 4

Concentrate on the Orcs and the Orcs with shields first. Keep moving to avoid arrows until you get the regular Orcs. Take out each archer with a fierce attack.

Floor 10

URUK-HAI MELEE X 6   URUK-HAI CROSSBOWMAN X 2

The Uruk-hai crossbowmen are deadly, especially if they throw their burning charges. Get them before you kill the others. But if you can't get away, fight through the regular Uruk-hai, then pick off the archers with your bow.

Floor 11

ORC ARCHER WITH EXPLODING ARROWS X 8

These archers fire deadly explosive charges, but they are in a formation that is easy to exploit. If you get between the archers, and dodge their shots, they shoot each other.

Floor 12

URUK-HAI MELEE X 2   ORC MELEE X 4   ORC ARCHER X 2

Make sure that the archers with explosive arrows are across the circle from you. Keep the middle tower between you and the archers. Staying behind the middle tower, peek out occasionally to shoot the two archers with arrows. Then kill the four Orcs and finish the two Uruk-hai with combos.

Floor 13

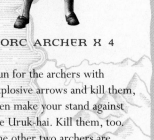

URUK-HAI MELEE X 4 **ORC ARCHER X 4**

Run for the archers with explosive arrows and kill them, then make your stand against the Uruk-hai. Kill them, too. The other two archers are across the circle. Use the middle tower as protection, then shoot them with arrows.

Floor 14

URUK-HAI MELEE X 4 **ORC WITH SHIELD X 2** **ORC ARCHER X 2**

Run for the first archer and kill him. Make your stand against the Orcs with shields and the Uruk-hai. Use the appropriate combos for those with shields and those without.

Floor 15

ORC ARCHER X 4 **CAVETROLL**

Run away from the cave-troll and pick off the archers one at a time with your sword. When they're gone, take down the cave-troll by dodging and counterattacking, or charging your fierce attack, lighting him on fire, then running away while he burns.

Floor 16

BERZERKER X 2 **ORC ARCHER X 2**

Avoid the Berzerkers and take out the archers first. Charge your fierce attack, set fire to them, and run to safety as they die.

FLOOR 17

URUK-HAI MELEE X 2 **BERZERKER X 2**

FOREST TROLL **ORC ARCHER X 2**

ORC ARCHER X 4

Get out of the forest trolls' range and eliminate the Orcs when you get an opportunity. When they're down, concentrate on individual forest trolls.

Get at least two of the archers first. If the other guys track you down, hit them with a fierce attack. Stay along the outside edge to get the archers, but fight the others when you get the chance.

FLOOR 18

BERZERKER **FOREST TROLL**

FLOOR 20

ORC ARCHER X 3 (ONE WITH EXPLODING ARROWS) **CAVE-TROLL**

ORC ARCHER X 4

FOREST TROLL X 2 **ORC WITH SHIELD X 2**

Get the archers first, but don't pass up a battle with the Berzerker if you can get it far away from the forest troll. Use R2 on the Berzerker when he's down, so he can't get up. When he and the archers are dead, take out the forst troll.

Run from the forest trolls and destroy the four archers. When they're gone, use your charged fierce attack to light the trolls on fire. You can kill them with three strikes.

FLOOR 19

ORC MELEE X 2 **CAVE-TROLL**

SECRET MISSION-LEGOLAS

TOWER OF ORTHANC

PLAYABLE CHARACTER

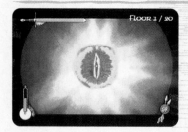

LEGOLAS

GOAL

- SURVIVE 20 FLOORS OF THE TOWER OF ORTHANC

IMPORTANT STRATEGY

start each floor by firing a few arrows at your enemies when they appear. you won't have time to choose your targets, so fire (even offscreen) three quick shots.

this strategy eliminates up to three foes before the action starts. use this strategy on every floor.

FLOOR 1

URUK-HAI SCOUT X 5

Run to a safe distance and use your arrows to plow through these Uruk-hai. You don't have to fight them up close.

FLOOR 2

URUK-HAI X 2   ORC WITH SHIELD X 4

Use fierce attacks to break up the shields. When the shields are gone, finish with your arrows.

Floor 3

URUK-HAI SCOUT X 2

ORC MELEE X 4

It's difficult to get clear of regular Orcs; fight some with your swords, but for the most part, use your arrows to make short work of these enemies.

Floor 4

URUK-HAI SCOUT X 3

ORC WITH SHIELD X 3

Destroy the three shields, then use your arrows to finish up. If there isn't room to use your bow, use sword combos.

Floor 5

ORC MELEE X 6

ORC WITH SHIELD X 3

Forget about your arrows on this level—the combat is in too close of quarters to make them useful. Swing your swords and unleash your best combos to make short work of these Orcs.

Floor 6

ORC ARCHER X 8

Don't get suckered into an archer duel. Instead, run and dodge around the outside of the circle, killing the archers one at a time.

Floor 7

URUK-HAI SCOUT X 2

ORC MELEE X 2

ORC ARCHER X 4

Run, dodge, and focus on the four Orc archers. When they're dead, use your bow to mop up.

FLOOR 8

ORC WITH SHIELD X 4   ORC ARCHER X 4

Get rid of the shields first, then dodge and fire arrows at anyone who's still alive.

FLOOR 9

ORC MELEE X 2   ORC WITH SHIELD X 2   ORC ARCHER X 4

First take out the Orcs and the Orcs with shields, then use your arrows to kill the four archers.

FLOOR 10

URUK-HAI MELEE X 6   URUK-HAI CROSSBOWMAN X 2

This is one of the most dangerous floors for Legolas. Let loose your best combos on the regular Uruk-hai first, but be wary of flammable grenades from the Uruk-hai crossbowmen. Fill your skill meter so you can quickly take out the armored Uruk-hai.

FLOOR 11

ORC ARCHER WITH EXPLODING ARROWS X 8

Run around and kill four of the archers with your swords or let them kill each other by accident. Once half are dead, pick off the others with your arrows.

FLOOR 12

URUK-HAI MELEE X 2   ORC MELEE X 4   ORC ARCHER X 2

Get free of the Uruk-hai and the Orcs, then target the archers. Every time you get free, fire an arrow to take someone out. If they catch you and knock you down, use your Rising Attack to create space so you can get free again.

Floor 13

URUK-HAI MELEE X 4 **ORC ARCHER X 4**

Run for two of the archers with explosive arrows; kill them. Fight to get free from the Uruk-hai, then use your arrows to light them ablaze. Slay the other two archers when you get the chance.

Floor 14

URUK-HAI MELEE X 4 **ORC WITH SHIELD X 2** **ORC ARCHER X 2**

Dash toward the first archer and kill him. Run from the Uruk-hai and shoot them with arrows. Use your fierce attack to de-shield the Orcs, then use arrows or combos to finish them off.

Floor 15

ORC ARCHER X 4 **CAVETROLL**

Run away from the cave-troll and pick off the archers one at a time with your sword. When they're dead, take the cave-troll out from a distance with your arrows.

Floor 16

BERZERKER X 2 **ORC ARCHER X 2**

Start with your bow pulled back (hold L1 and ✗). When you see a Berzerker, release ✗ and nail him with an arrow. Pick off the other Berzerker and two archers.

FLOOR 17

URUK-HAI MELEE X 2

BERZERKER X 2

ORC ARCHER X 4

First get one of the Berzerkers with your arrows. If you don't, you have to fight out from in between two Berzerkers and two Uruk-hai with archers.

FLOOR 18

BERZERKER

FOREST TROLL

ORC ARCHER X 4

Get free from the Berzerker and the forest troll, then kill the archers. Eliminate the Berzerker with an arrow. Take out the forest troll with one fierce attack, then run away. He can't be hurt by your arrows.

FLOOR 19

ORC MELEE X 2

ORC ARCHER X 2

CAVE-TROLL

FOREST TROLL

Get out of the cave-trolls range and destroy any of the Orcs when you get an opportunity. When they're down, take out the darker cave-troll with your arrows, then slay the lighter one by conventional means.

FLOOR 20

ORC ARCHER X 3 (ONE WITH EXPLODING ARROWS)

CAVE-TROLL

FOREST TROLL X 2

ORC WITH SHIELD X 2

Run from the cave-trolls, then kill the four archers. When they're dead, target the dark cave-troll with arrows, then kill the other two with your sword.

SECRET MISSION-GIMLI

TOWER OF ORTHANC

PLAYABLE CHARACTER

GOAL

- SURVIVE 20 FLOORS OF THE TOWER OF ORTHANC

GIMLI

IMPORTANT STRATEGY

start each floor by running away from the middle, charging up your sword before the enemies appear, and unleashing an attack on whoever's nearest to you. If you purchased wrath of moria, you'll set fire to multiple foes.

This takes out a few of your foes before the action starts. This strategy isn't repeated every time, but you should use it on each floor.

FLOOR 1

URUK-HAI SCOUT X 5

Unleash Balin's combos or use the Bane of Saruman (■, ✕, R2) to take out these guys.

FLOOR 2

URUK-HAI SCOUT X 2   ORC WITH SHIELD X 4

Wade into the middle of the battle and take out the guys with shields using Balin's Judgment (▲, ▲, ●, ▲).

FLOOR 3

URUK-HAI SCOUT X 2   ORC MELEE X 4

Wade into the middle of these foes and use your combos to make them suffer.

FLOOR 4

URUK-HAI SCOUT X 3   **ORC WITH SHIELD X 3**

Smash the three shields, then use your combos on the remaining enemies. If you build your skill meter, this is easier.

FLOOR 5

ORC MELEE X 3   **ORC WITH SHIELD X 3**

Use Balin's Judgment or Deliverance to kill the Orcs with shields. Use the other combos on the regular Orcs.

FLOOR 6

ORC ARCHER X 8

Run around the outside of the circle, dodge the enemies, and kill the archers one at a time. Keep moving so you do not take needless damage.

FLOOR 7

URUK-HAI SCOUT X 2   **ORC MELEE X 2**   **ORC ARCHER X 4**

Kill the Orcs and the Uruk-hai quickly, then dispatch the archers. Don't get between two archers, or you'll suffer damage.

FLOOR 8

ORC WITH SHIELD X 4   **ORC ARCHER X 4**

Target the Orc archers first, but if the Orcs with shields hassle you, fight them to buy yourself some breathing room.

SECRET MISSION—GIMLI

Floor 9

ORC MELEE X 2   **ORC WITH SHIELD X 2**   **ORC ARCHER X 4**

Focus on the Orcs and the Orcs with shields first. Avoid arrows until you've gotten the regular Orcs, then take out the archers with your axe.

Floor 10

URUK-HAI MELEE X 6   **URUK-HAI CROSSBOWMAN X 2**

Get the crossbowmen before killing the others. If you can't get away, fight through the regular Uruk-hai, then deal with the archers. Watch out for explosive grenades.

Floor 11

ORC ARCHER WITH EXPLODING ARROWS X 8

These archers fire deadly explosive charges; be careful and try to get them to shoot each other. Duck and weave as you take them out.

Floor 12

URUK-HAI MELEE X 2   **ORC MELEE X 4**   **ORC ARCHER X 2**

Stay across the circle from the archers; keep the middle tower in between you and them. Kill the four Orcs, then finish the two Uruk-hai with combos. Hunt down and kill the archers.

Floor 13

URUK-HAI MELEE X 4   **ORC ARCHER X 4**

Slay the archers with explosive arrows, then fight and kill the Uruk-hai. When you're done, take out the other two archers across the circle.

FLOOR 14

URUK-HAI MELEE X 4

ORC WITH SHIELD X 2

ORC ARCHER X 2

Get one of the archers, then fight the rest of the melee troop using your best combos. Afterward, take out the remaining archer.

FLOOR 15

ORC ARCHER X 4

CAVE-TROLL

Run away from the cave-troll and individually pick off the archers with your axe. After you kill them, charge your fierce attack and torch the cave-troll when he gets close.

FLOOR 16

BERZERKER X 2

ORC ARCHER X 2

Attack the Berzerkers; use R2 to knock them down. You may take some damage from the archers' arrows, but you'll be fine. Finish the archers when the Berzerkers are dead.

FLOOR 17

URUK-HAI MELEE X 2

BERZERKER X 2

ORC ARCHER X 4

Get at least two of the archers first. Stay alongside the outside edge and pick them off as you travel around the circle. If the other enemies catch you, fight them using all of your combos.

SECRET MISSION—GIMLI

Floor 18

BERZERKER

FOREST TROLL

ORC ARCHER X 4

Run to kill the archers, but stay out of range of the Berzerker and the forest troll. If the Berzerker catches you, fight him. When the archers and the Berzerker are dead, take out the forest troll using your charged fierce attack.

Floor 19

ORC MELEE X 2

ORC ARCHER X 2

CAVE-TROLL

FOREST TROLL

Get out of the cave-trolls' range, then kill the Orcs when an opportunity arises. When they're down, concentrate on one cave-troll at a time.

Floor 20

ORC ARCHER X 3
(ONE WITH
EXPLODING ARROWS)

CAVE-TROLL

FOREST TROLL X 2

ORC WITH
SHIELD X 2

Run from the cave-trolls while attacking the four archers. When they're gone, use your charged fierce attack to light each cave-troll on fire. Do this quickly so you'll take less damage.

When you finish, you face Saruman. Again, you don't have to fight him.

SECRET MISSION-ISILDUR

TOWER OF ORTHANC

GOAL

- SURVIVE 20 FLOORS OF THE TOWER OF ORTHANC

IMPORTANT STRATEGY

start every floor by running away from the middle, charging up your sword before the enemies appear, and unleashing an attack on whomever's nearest to you. you'll set fire to multiple foes.

PLAYABLE CHARACTER

ISILDUR

Isildur is the character that you unlock after beating a secret mission with any of the other characters. He has the same skills Aragorn has.

Follow Aragorn's strategy, and you'll make it through this difficult special mission.

After you finish this mission, go back and play the previous levels as Isildur. It's great fun to take down the now-simple enemies of the early levels with this powered-up character.

CODES

If you want a change of pace from the regular gameplay in *The Lord of the Rings: The Two Towers* or help to get you through some of the difficult levels, use the following cheats.

Entering Cheats

To enter cheats, do the following:

1. Start playing any of the missions.
2. Pause the game by hitting START.
3. While the game is paused, press and hold all four shoulder buttons: R1 + L1 + R2 + L2.
4. Enter a code while holding down the four shoulder buttons.
5. A metal-clashing sound signals when you've entered a proper code.
6. Release the shoulder buttons and hit START to continue your mission.

Anytime Cheat Codes

Restore Health
▲, ⇩, ✕, ⇧

This code immediately boosts your health to 100 percent.

Restore Missiles
✕, ⇩, ▲, ⇧

This code refills your ranged attack ammo up to the highest amount you can carry.

+1,000 Experience
✕, ⇩, ⇩, ⇩

Add 1,000 experience points to your post-mission score. Use this as many times as you want.

Level Two Skills
●, ⇨, ●, ⇨

This code automatically gives you all of the level two skills.

Level Four Skills
▲, ⇧, ▲, ⇧

This code automatically gives you all of the level four skills.

Level Six Skills
■, ⇦, ■, ⇦

This code automatically gives you all of the level six skills.

Level Eight Skills
✕, ✕, ⇩, ⇩

This code automatically gives you all of the level eight skills.

Reward Cheat Codes

> ### NOTE
> These codes only work after you finish the game and open the codes menu.

Always Devastating
■, ■, ●, ●

This code makes your melee weapon continually glow and cause double damage as if your skill meter was completely full.

All Skills
▲, ●, ▲, ●

This code gives your character every one of the skills he can earn.

Mini-Enemies
▲, ▲, ✕, ✕

This shrinks all the enemies. Hit the code again to return them to normal.

Infinite Missiles
■, ●, ✕, ▲

You'll never run out of ranged attack ammo when using this code.

Slo-Mo
▲, ●, ✕, ■

This code slows down the action. It looks cool and helps you get through tough situations.

Invulnerable
▲, ■, ✕, ●

No matter how hard the attack, you won't take any damage while using this code.

EXTRAS

THE BONUS FEATURES

Even if you've played all the way through *The Lord of the Rings: The Two Towers* with all three regular characters, plus the secret character Isildur, you still haven't seen everything this game has to offer.

Look at the mission screen to find many cool unlockable featurettes. As you play through the game's missions and build each of your characters to level 10, these open for you. Check them out.

INTERVIEW: PETER JACKSON AND BARRIE OSBORNE

The movie creators talk about the film and the game.

INTERVIEW: ELIJAH WOOD

The young star talks about playing Frodo in *The Lord of the Rings* video game.

INTERVIEW: IAN MCKELLEN

Sir Ian talks about playing Gandalf in *The Lord of the Rings* video game.

THE LORD OF THE RINGS: THE MAKING OF THE VIDEO GAME

This is a behind-the-scenes look at how *The Lord of the Rings: The Two Towers* was made.

THE LORD OF THE RINGS: CONCEPT ART

You'll see art inspired by *The Lord of the Rings* from John Howe and Alan Lee.

ROHAN AND HELM'S DEEP PRODUCTION PHOTOS

Photographs of characters and scenery from Rohan and Helm's Deep.

INTERVIEW: VIGGO MORTENSEN

Viggo Mortensen talks about playing Aragorn in *The Lord of the Rings* video game.

FANGORN AND ORTHANC PRODUCTION PHOTOS

Photographs of characters and scenery from Fangorn and Orthanc.

INTERVIEW: ORLANDO BLOOM

Orlando Bloom talks about playing Legolas in *The Lord of the Rings* video game.

THE FELLOWSHIP OF THE RING PRODUCTION PHOTOS

Photographs show characters and scenery from *The Fellowship of the Ring*.

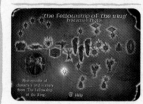

INTERVIEW: JOHN RHYS-DAVIES

John Rhys-Davies talks about playing Gimli in *The Lord of the Rings* video game.